What scholars

MW00778340

What Women Want

"Alexander and Bowers allow Church of God women to express their hopes and fears, and the results are both powerful and enlightening. Their study effectively debunks a number of myths, including the belief that a liberal theological agenda is driving the debate. Rather, Church of God women are conservative, called, and confident, wishing only to fulfill the God-given mandate upon their lives. I predict that the statistics and analysis of this book will reverberate through the Church of God and the American Pentecostal world. May we have the ears to hear what the Spirit is saying to the churches."

—DALE COULTER
PhD, Associate Professor of Historical Theology, Regent University

"This presents a serious challenge to Church of God leaders and pastors to hear our sisters in the faith and affirm their calling and gifts. The Spirit has been poured out upon all flesh and we must be willing to prepare the way for the voices of Spirit-filled sisters."

—REV. DAN TOMBERLIN
DMin, Director of Student Placement, Pentecostal Theological Seminary

"This significant work illumines the lives, dreams, frustrations and ultimately the hopes of a generation of Church of God women. Examining the class, racial, and ethnic diversity of this denomination's women ministers is sorely needed for today's church. This fascinating and timely study offers a voice to women as they navigate their calling in the midst of resistance."

—ARLENE SANCHEZ WALSH
PhD, Associate Professor of Church History, Latino/a Studies, Azusa Pacific University

"Acts 2:16–21 outlines our Pentecostal worldview and strategy for global evangelization. It is the declaration of the mission of God, that all who call on his name will be saved. The way they will hear is through the prophetic voice of men *and* women, old *and* young, of all classes and people groups. This declaration of the co-mission of the church set the stage for Paul to declare, 'there is neither Jew nor Greek, bond nor free, male nor female, we are all one in Christ Jesus.' I commend James and Kimberly and the leaders of the Church of God for taking an honest assessment of the current reality. This isn't about equal rights, but about a harvest that is ready, and the laborers cannot be one half of the workforce. We must have all hands on deck in order to fulfill the mission. Our roles and responsibilities must be determined by God's call and gifting, not ambition or cultural biases. We are better together!"

—REV. TAMMY DUNAHOO
General Supervisor, The Foursquare Church

"*Finally* someone has asked Pentecostal women ministers the right questions and stopped long enough to listen. The result is a book that gives a voice to women with a sense of calling who need and want support, affirmation, opportunity, and equitable compensation—in short, to be taken as seriously as any man would be in living out that call.

"In analyzing survey responses from 726 of the 3088 licensed Church of God women in ministers (in 2012), Alexander and Bowers have provided a remarkable 'reality-based context' that shatters myths, tells a story, and sets a stage for a 'renewed vision of a relationship' where men and women can move past bad theology and 'get on with the business of the kingdom.'

"This book rekindles my hope for the future of women in ministry—a hope first nurtured by my own Pentecostal pastor father who provided ministry opportunities for me, encouraged me, and instilled confidence in my life as a teenage girl with a sense of calling to serve the church. May more of our brothers see, listen and act as he did."

—DR. LOIS E. OLENA
Associate Professor of Practical Theology and Jewish Studies, Assemblies of God Theological Seminary; Executive Director, Society for Pentecostal Studies

"There is a greeting in a Zulu tribe in South Africa that is translated 'I see you,' followed by a common response of 'I am here.' I am so thankful that Kimberly E. Alexander and James P. Bowers have had the courage to write such a timely book as *What Women Want*. Their research reveals that what women in the church want is simply to be seen and celebrated as the gifts of God that they are. They don't want to be invisible or held back because of their gender. They don't want to have to go outside of the church to soar and fulfill their God-given destinies, but they are struggling to find a place within the church to spread out their wings.

"*What Women Want* is a wake up call to the church as a whole, even beyond Pentecostal circles. It is an invitation for Christians in leadership to reflect on what is being preached from the pulpit to see if it is actually happening in practice. It is a challenge to seek to listen and understand what is really going on in the hearts of our brothers and sisters. It is a call to reflect on core beliefs. It presents an opportunity for the church to step into even more of the fullness of what it is destined to be.

"Safe places need to be created to hear what is really going on with the women in our congregations. The church is at a crossroads. By initiating the dialogue and creating space for women's voices to be heard, I hope and pray along with Alexander and Bowers that, from this research, change will come for the 'good of the church, the advancement of the Kingdom and the glory of God.'"

—JENNIFER A. MISKOV
PhD, Founding Director of Silver to Gold and Destiny House

"This is the first empirical study on this topic in our tradition. The fact that it is an empirical study helps move discussions about the role of women in ministry beyond the visceral level and provides a systematic point of departure for examining the issue from a different angle. In doing this, it gets the conversation out of the emotional eddy in which it has been trapped."

—BOB L. JOHNSON JR.
PhD, Professor and Program Coordinator, Department of Educational Leadership and Policy, The University of Alabama

"Finally, a book that speaks about the desires of Pentecostal women working in and desiring to be in egalitarian positions with the church. *What Women Want* relays what women really want when it comes to their ministry and their position in the church. Even though this book is drawn from the women in ministry in the Church of God, it could be a book written from the testimony of any number of denominations. I found myself in some of the testimonies and felt tears of understanding welling up in my eyes. *What Women Want* is cutting edge in that it records the testimony of contemporary women working in the ministry and trying to find their voice in the administration of the church. No longer speaking through others, but actually speaking their own mind, Pentecostal women are speaking candidly about their desires for the church."

—DR. CANDACE C. SHIELDS
Chaplain, San Bernardino, California

What Women Want

What Women Want

Pentecostal Women Ministers Speak for Themselves

KIMBERLY ERVIN ALEXANDER
and
JAMES P. BOWERS

Foreword by
ESTRELDA Y. ALEXANDER

WIPF & STOCK · Eugene, Oregon

WHAT WOMEN WANT
Pentecostal Women Ministers Speak for Themselves

Wipf & Stock
An Imprint of Wipf and Stock Publishers
199 W. 8th Ave., Suite 3
Eugene, OR 97401

www.wipfandstock.com

PAPERBACK ISBN: 978-1-5326-4375-0
HARDCOVER ISBN: 978-1-5326-4376-7
EBOOK ISBN: 978-1-5326-4377-4

Manufactured in the U.S.A.   02/12/19

Previously published by The Seymour Press (Laurel, MD), 2013

This book is dedicated,
lovingly and hopefully,
to our daughters:

Jamie Lauren Bowers

and

Doris Hope Alexander Butcher
Emma Catherine Alexander Back
Leslie Jeannine Alexander

Contents

Graphs and Charts

Contributors

Kimberly Ervin Alexander, Assoc. Professor of the History of Christianity, Regent University School of Divinity, Virginia Beach, VA

James P. Bowers, Director of Graduate Studies, Professor of Practical Theology and Formation, Virginia Bible College, Dumfries, VA

Mireya Alvarez, Vice-President for Academic Affairs, Asian Seminary of Christian Ministries, Makati City, Philippines

Paulette Davis, Hospice Chaplain, Saad's Hospice Service, Mobile, AL

Sabrina Evans, Clinical Mental Health Counselor, Missionary, Prague, Czech Republic

Peggy Madden Harmann, Chaplain, Cookeville Regional Medical Center, Cookeville, TN

Diane Mann, Pastor, 4th Avenue International Worship Center, Ft. Lauderdale, FL

Mia Pittman-Head, Pastor, Omega Harvest Church, Red Bank, TN

Contributors

David G. Roebuck, Director, Hal Bernard Dixon, Jr. Pentecostal Research Center; Assistant Professor, Lee University, Church of God Historian, Cleveland, TN

Emily Brown Stone, Assoc. Professor, Marriage and Family Therapy, Pfeiffer University, Misenheimer, NC

Mary Ruth (Morris) Stone, Retired; former International Coordinator of Women's Ministries, Church of God and Director of Faculty Development, Lee University, Cleveland, TN

Cynthia Woolever, Research Director of US Congregations Project, Presbyterian Church (USA), Louisville, KY

Foreword

ESTRELDA Y. ALEXANDER, PHD
President, William Seymour College

AT ITS 2010 GENERAL Assembly, the all-male General Council of the Church of God (Cleveland, TN) voted, once again, to withhold the possibility of fully empowered ordination[1] from women clergy within the denomination. In a subsequent session of the Society for Pentecostal Studies, denominational scholars met to wrestle with how they might support a push toward an affirmative vote on the issue.

At this session, orchestrated by Dr. Dale Coulter and me, not surprisingly the majority of those present were fully ordained men —called "Ordained Bishops" in the Church of God—who serve out their ministry calling within the academy. There were significantly fewer women present and only a small number of these held clergy credentials. More interestingly, most of the discussion involved our male colleagues and most of the women in the room said little.

A number of proposals came to the floor. Given the history of repeated defeat at moving the issue forward, however, none of them seemed particularly appealing or potentially effective. At the end of the session, there was no consensus except that something

---

1. See Mark Chaves's exceptional work, *Ordaining Women*.

more needed to be done. Yet, it was obvious to some of us that an important element in the struggle to gain equity for women clergy was missing from our deliberation. If we were to make genuine progress in this arena, it was imperative to understand what it is that women really want.

What do women want? That question is very important. Moreover, it might seem that within the Christian church that is more than 2000 years old and a denomination that is more than 125 years old, the issue might have been settled. Yet, within the evangelical Christian context, the question—to which women do not fully contribute in framing the ongoing discussion—and the issue of their place in the ministry and leadership of the church remains unsettled.

Moreover, beyond the group of scholars gathered for the Society for Pentecostal Studies session, there is no real consensus about the legitimacy of the issue. There is no consensus regarding what women clergy want—or ought to want—from the church. On one hand, some see any push for women's greater involvement in denominational leadership and government as a rebellion against authority. Some still see any discussion of any "rights" for women as a failure to understand biblical models of servant leadership and a capitulation to secular feminist movements. Indeed, the very attempt to answer the question is unsettling to many. On the other hand, some see women's accommodation to existing systems that limit their participation as capitulation to sinful structures of oppression.

In this work, Kimberly Alexander (a historical theologian, past seminary assistant vice-president and former president of the Society for Pentecostal Studies) and James Bowers (past seminary vice-president, former pastor and expert in spiritual formation of clergy) have taken the extraordinary step of allowing women to speak for themselves. They have attempted to lift up their concerns and to do so within the context of a Pentecostal denomination that has historically limited women's participation in critical areas of leadership. In so doing, they have given voice to women who express their deepest joys, concerns, and hopes for themselves and the church they love.

The women in this volume speak with a clarity and conviction that is unmistakable. For more than a century, they have been silenced within many levels of the life of the denomination. They have been unable to use their voices in the General Council of the General Assembly, where they are locked out of the voting process. They have been unable to use their voices fully in the local assembly where they have, until 2010, historically been restricted from service on church councils. Further, they have often been unable to use their voices or talents for leadership outside the local congregation since they are prohibited, for the most part, from serving in state or national positions of authority in the USA. In reality, they have even been unable to speak as pastoral leaders of viable congregations, since most placements to existing congregations are reserved for men, and women are primarily limited to church planting.

The voices of young women, older women, black women, white women, Hispanic women, urban and rural women, some with theological training and some without training, are included in this work. They share a common, undeniable sense of call and a desire to serve their church to their fullest capacity, to be acknowledged and fairly compensated for their contribution, and to have their male colleagues treat them as full ministry partners with all the rights and privileges inherent in that status.

Wherever there has been a need, these women have been willing—indeed, have felt compelled to serve. And it is precisely their unswerving sense of call that has led them to establish and pastor local churches in some of the most difficult circumstances imaginable, has led them to the mission field to serve in harsh circumstances in remote places and has driven them to faithfully serve in a variety of parachurch ministry settings, often with little material compensation. As pastors, evangelists, missionaries, chaplains, and Christian educators, they have made an incalculable contribution to the kingdom that certainly has not received the appreciation it deserves.

After suffering in silence for so long, some have left the Pentecostal movement to go where they believed they would have more freedom. While they could have chosen to do the same, the women highlighted in this volume have remained faithful in a denomination that has failed to be faithful or as supportive to them as it could have been. More remarkably, they have asked for little in return. They have launched no public protest. There have been no demands laid down. There have been no boycotts.

Answering the question of what women want is a crucial first step for working for gender equity within the evangelical and Pentecostal communities. Yet another important question is why women stay in faith communities where such equity is not present. The reasons—and there are many—as revealed in the words of testimonies of women such as those within this volume may surprise us. Yet, answering that question is another crucial step in correcting the inequitable systems in which they live out their Christian witness.

While the findings offered in this book are specifically about the experiences of women in the Church of God, they could be about women in many Pentecostal denominations or many segments of the broader Evangelical faith community. Indeed, they could be about any woman who has felt the call by God to Christian ministry, but whose denomination has denied her the opportunity and support to fully carry out that call.

In the end, what women who are called to actively serve in ministry want is to have their calling taken seriously by the church and to be treated as if their ministry matters. They want the opportunity to speak for themselves and to be heard at every level of the church. For when we listen to them with open hearts, their situations and the stories behind them are compelling.

Acknowledgments

THERE ARE MANY PERSONS whose support, encouragement and consultation helped make this research project on Pentecostal women ministers in the Church of God a reality. Estrelda Alexander, Dale Coulter, Mark Cartledge, and David Roebuck were important dialogue partners and provided helpful insights on the research design and process. Raymond Culpepper, Lynn Stone, Julian Robinson, Dan Tomberlin, and Robert Newman were helpful in providing access to information essential to conducting the project. Sarah Parnell, Regent University graduate assistant, and Randy Turpin assisted with preparation of the manuscript for publication. Cynthia Woolever was an invaluable consultant and analyst from outside the Church of God. Joshua Butcher perfectly captured the revelatory nature of this work in his cover design of the original publication. Linda Ambrose, Bob Johnson, and Michael Wilkinson provided helpful feedback on the research methodology, results and analysis. Finally, great gratitude and appreciation is due the hundreds of Church of God women ministers who completed the research survey and poured out their hearts with stories that moved us to tears and motivated us to complete this journey.

Abbreviations

AB	Administrative Bishop
CAMS	Callings and Ministry Studies
CIMS	Certificate in Ministerial Studies
COG	Church of God
CPLC	Center for Pentecostal Leadership and Care
EL	Exhorter's License
GA	General Assembly
GC	General Council
MAP	Ministerial Affirmation Program
MIP	Ministerial Internship Program
NAE	National Association of Evangelicals
OB	Ordained Bishop
OM	Ordained Minister
PCG	Pastoral Covenant Group
WIM	Women in Ministry

Chapter 1

Hearing Their Voices

What do women want? Has anyone ever asked
women in the Church of God what they really want?
—Estrelda Alexander

WHY THIS STUDY OF PENTECOSTAL WOMEN MINISTERS?

JPB: After returning from the 2010 Church of God (COG; in Cleveland, TN) General Assembly (GA) highlighted by an Internet streamed debate by Ordained Bishops (OBs; all male) in General Council (GC) sessions on a measure that would allow women ministers to also serve as OBs, I was confronted over breakfast by my then-fifteen-year-old daughter, Jamie. She began tactfully. "Dad, I don't want to upset you, but after what I saw on the Internet when the General Assembly discussed women ministers, you need to know I'm probably not going to be COG when I grow up." I told her I understood and that I hoped she would live to see things change and would be a Pentecostal Christian whether she was COG or not.

Given the distasteful and disrespectful rhetoric of the web-streamed debate by male ministers—even though there were certainly more reasonable voices—despite the pained feeling inside, I could hardly argue with her.

KEA: Seated as closely to the GC seating as was allowable for women, I was joined by female colleagues, students, and former students. Many of these women were already credentialed; others were in the discerning process as to whether or not they should be licensed in the COG, the church of their tradition and heritage. I felt not only my own pain at hearing the debates and arguments, but the pain of these young women, whose future and destiny were being discussed by men, most of whom did not know them, many of whom had less education and theological training than they did. I began to receive texts from my daughters, who were watching the live-stream from other states. Their immediate concern was for me: "Are you alright?" Their further texts, like the words of my colleagues and students, revealed pain and then anger. For them and for my son-in-law, trained in the COG seminary where I was on the faculty, this debate and decision was the final straw. As my son-in-law, a pastor, said, "I'm leaving my home denomination not because of what it can or cannot do for my own ministry, but because it will not fully affirm the ministry of my daughter."

As we left the floor, breaking for lunch, the young women surrounding me wept. Many male ministers offered support and concern while too many others gave us triumphant glances and scornful smirks. One seasoned woman minister and educator, the wife of a prominent male minister and mother of another, quickly walked away in grief, saying, "I can't talk about this right now."

DURING THE 2011 SOCIETY for Pentecostal Studies meeting held in Memphis, Tennessee, a group of Pentecostal scholars mostly affiliated with the COG met to consider whether and how they should respond to the most recent rebuff of the full empowerment of women ministers in the COG GA in August the previous year. Following an open discussion among approximately seventy-five Society attendees of possible factors influencing the lack of greater official affirmation of women ministers, a consensus emerged that an empirical study was needed to more adequately understand how women think about the issue of fuller endorsement and to determine what is the nature of their ministry experience. One of this study's principal investigators (JPB) was asked by the group to explore the possibility of having such research authorized by COG denominational leaders.

MYTHBUSTER:

COG leadership has adequately studied the role and issues of women ministers.

No COG commissioned study or empirical research of women's ministry has been conducted.

Subsequent conversation with the General Overseer of the COG, Raymond Culpepper, did not lead to any official commissioning of the research, but did result in the granting of access to denominational ministerial databases, the assurance that no COG polity or policies would be violated by the research, and promises of sufficient cooperation that a study could be conducted on women ministers and issues affecting their vocation within the denomination.[1] With these assurances, a research project design began to be developed in dialogue with other scholars and researchers to be implemented during one of the primary researcher's (JPB) Sabbatical as a Visiting Scholar at Duke University School of Divinity during the 2011–2012 academic year, and with the assistance of COG historical theologian Kimberly Ervin Alexander. The purpose of the research would be to hear directly from women concerning their attitudes about achieving full equality with their male ministerial colleagues, learn more about their ministry expe-

1. Interestingly, once the first email notices were sent to women ministers inviting them to complete a survey, notice came that the women in ministry survey was "not approved by the General Overseer." Respondents subsequently received reiteration of the independent nature of the research project to clarify any possible misunderstanding that the survey was prepared or specifically approved by the COG headquarters.

rience, and identify recommendations for better supporting women who serve in Pentecostal ministry within the COG. Of course, denominational debates in the COG GC excluded women's voices, and even in the GA—which includes women—male ministers often trump the input of women with parliamentary maneuvers or political rhetoric.

Giving voice to COG women ministers was a major goal, but it was also believed that research findings might illumine the challenges and opportunities for Pentecostal women ministers in other contexts. That the women ministers surveyed for this research *all* serve in the COG has been noted as a limitation. Given the strong affirmation these COG women ministers made of their Pentecostal identity through self-description, hermeneutical orientation and spirituality, we would argue not that they can speak for their sisters, but they can and do testify of the same Spirit-given calling, gifting, and grace.

To our knowledge, no empirical research has been conducted that allows Pentecostal women ministers to speak for themselves. While there are important social and cultural forces impacting gender roles that need to be analyzed, nothing more than a cursory acknowledgement of these influences lies within the scope of this project. Research findings reported in this book focus on the expressed views of women with the hope that greater understanding, support, and affirmation of Pentecostal women ministers will result.

HOW CAME WE HERE?

The COG (Cleveland, TN) stands in the Holiness-Pentecostal trajectory of North American Pentecostalism. Though its roots go back to an organizational meeting in 1886, called by Baptist preacher R. G. Spurling, a revival in 1896 imprinted the church with the Holiness Movement's expectation of sanctification as a subsequent experience to the new birth. Many reportedly spoke in tongues at that same meeting and in the ensuing years. The church intersected with the Azusa Street Revival in early 1908 when its persuasive leader, Ambrose Jessup Tomlinson, was baptized in the Holy Spirit at a Sunday morning service in which G. B. Cashwell, adherent of the "Apostolic Faith" of the Los Angeles revival, preached a sermon and gave an invitation for Spirit baptism.

MYTHBUSTER:

Full equality of men and women in ministry is a liberal view and a result of worldliness encroaching upon the church.

The earliest records indicate that full equality is actually the *conservative* position to be taken.

In line with many other Holiness and Pentecostal churches of that era, numerous references to "men and women" can be found in the COG Minutes and in the writings of Tomlinson.[2]

Tomlinson wrote in *The Last Great Conflict*, "It is our purpose to encourage both men and women, young and old; to undertake great things for God and expect great things from God."[3]

Even prior to Tomlinson's Pentecostal experience, there were discussions about the ordination of women as deaconesses and evangelists. Ministerial credentials issued and signed by Tomlinson, as early as 1909 and as late as 1914, authorized men and women to "publish, preach and defend the Gospel of Jesus Christ, to baptize, to administer the Lord's Supper and the washing of the Saints[sic] feet. Though there is no evidence that women performed all such ministerial functions, it may be argued that at this point there was the highest degree of parity. Additionally, in 1908, discussion at the assembly affirmed the call of women to the diaconate:

> Deaconesses and their duties: Discussed at some length and decided that women are qualified and feel the call to the work as outlined in Rom 16:2 in connection with Acts 6:3 which indicates that she is a female Deacon, therefore her work is similar to that of a Deacon, should

2. See *Minutes of the Church of God General Assembly 1912, 1914.*
3. Tomlinson, *Last Great Conflict*, vii.

5

be appointed by the Church to exercise such qualities as she is gifted with. We further recommend her as the woman mentioned in Titus 2:3–5 which duty she should exercise as directed by the Spirit. Also she may along with the elder men, take her part of 1 Peter 5:1–4.[4]

As has been discussed at length elsewhere, the implications of this statement are significant.[5]

There seems to be a consensus that the testimony of call and giftedness are the primary basis for affirmation and appointment of women to ministry and that women "should exercise [their gifts] as directed by the Spirit . . . along with the elder men." However, one year later there is a capitulation to a prevalent view held by those in non-Holiness or Pentecostal traditions that women may serve in the diaconate only if their husbands are deacons.[6]

MYTHBUSTER:

COG forefathers drew their view of women in ministry from their study of Scripture.

COG leaders mirrored the prevailing limitations on women found in the non-Holiness or Pentecostal churches in their region.

By at least as early as 1912, Tomlinson and another prominent minister, M. S. Lemons, began espousing their interpretation of Paul's admonition for women to keep silent in church settings, a unique view that understood "church" to be synonymous with the "church meeting to transact business." This bifurcation of church/business from worship has been shown to have lasting import for

4. *Original Handwritten Minutes Typescript 3rd General Assembly (1908)*, 4.

5. See Alexander and Bowers, "Race and Gender Equality," 131–51.

6. Baptists in the region subscribed to a subordinate role for women serving in the diaconate. "Adoption of the 'Deaconess' language implied women were authorized to serve based on their husband's call and office and were subordinate to male 'Deacons.'" See comments on the work of Tennessee Baptist minister R. B. C. Howell's 1846 work, *The Deaconship: Its Nature, Qualifications, Relations, Duties* in Alexander and Bowers, "Race and Gender Equality," 145–46 and 147n7.

the place and contribution of women to the COG. The result was that women could be recognized as charismatically gifted and could speak prophetically from the pulpit, and could even serve as pastors of local churches, but have no voice in the "business," leadership or administration of the church.

COG historian David Roebuck has shown that, from this early period, there was an evolution (or a devolution) of the understanding of the role and function, as well as nomenclature, for women ministers.[7] Roebuck's research demonstrates that there was a growing segregation between male and women ministers as early as 1914, but with an escalation beginning in 1931. At that point, women ministers began to be listed in separate categories from other ranks, such as Deacon, Evangelists and Bishops.

A major contributor to the view of women's participation in the COG came from the rising influence of Evangelical and Fundamentalist interpretations of certain texts, often ignoring context and taking a non-narrative approach. The Tomlinsonian interpretation was fortified for the COG by its close association with those in Evangelical churches. As the COG and other classical Pentecostal denominations embraced the Evangelical movement, most conspicuously by joining forces in 1948 with the formation of the National Association of Evangelicals (NAE), so too it adopted its view of family and women's roles.

Interestingly, in 1948, the year of the NAE charter, the nomenclature for ministerial ranks in the COG changed. The rank of Evangelist was eliminated and the rank of Licensed Minister was instituted. However, women's credentials remained unchanged; women were "granted Evangelist's Certificates."[8]

At this point, in lists of ministers, all women ministers beyond the novice rank of Exhorter are listed separately. "Licensed Ministers" lists included males only. Roebuck notes that the minutes of the assembly include this summary: "'It is understood that the ministerial status of lady evangelists remains unchanged.'"[9]

7. See Appendix 1.

8. Roebuck, "I Have Done," 399.

9. *Minutes of the 42nd General Assembly (1948)*, 27, cited in Roebuck,

The implication of this move was that the Assembly did not want to silence the charismatic call of the woman who was an evangelist, but she was not recognized as professional clergy. Tomlinson's legacy lived on in these later developments. His statements of 1915 were paraphrased and voiced in 1948 and the years following: "Let the good sisters feel at perfect liberty to preach the gospel, pray for the sick or well, testify, exhort, etc., but humbly hold themselves aloof from taking charge of the governmental affairs."[10]

According to Roebuck, the GA of 1958 made official the designation "women minister." The primary responsibilities of these women were limited to those involving proclamation, and though they were allowed to serve as pastors, they were to do so "under the supervision of the district pastor" and without sacerdotal authority. By 1964, women ministers were referred to as "Lady Ministers" and in 1972 the nomenclature "Lady Evangelist" appeared on credentials issued by the denomination to women. Roebuck's research indicates that this was done without official action or ratification by the Executive Committee, Executive Council or by the GA.[11] In effect, this means that language determining the identity and status of women in ministry was altered in a manner detrimental to the full empowerment of women without appropriate authorization by the highest governing body of the denomination, the GA.[12]

In 1994, however, the first real challenge to Tomlinson's view was seen in the redefining of the understanding of the constituency

---

"Limiting Liberty," 160.

10. Tomlinson, "Paul's Statements Considered", 4.

11. Roebuck, "Limiting Liberty," 164.

12. See Gause, *Church of God Polity*. Gause writes, "The highest court of authority in the Church of God is the General Assembly" (*Church of God Polity*, 73). He continues, "All auxiliaries of the Church of God are under the supervision of the General Assembly. Their purposes, government, methods, officers and members are subject to the review and approval of the General Assembly" (*Church of God Polity*, 78). For the most recent statement of the responsibilities and powers of the General Assembly, see "Bylaws of the Church of God."

gender of the GA. In that year, it was decided that the GA, consisted of all members present, male and *female*, over the age of 16. A few years later, in 2000, the title of the second rank of licensure for COG ministers was changed to "Ordained Minister," (OM) in effect, granting ordination to women. However, women were still excluded from the highest rank, now called "Ordained Bishop" (OB). It is this rank which grants men entrance into the body known as the GC, consisting of all OBs present at the biennial assembly. This council also comprises those who are eligible for leadership and administrative oversight positions in the denomination and sets the agenda for changes in polity, all of which are ratified by the gender inclusive GA, consisting of all eligible COG members present. This "stained glass ceiling" now prevents women direct access and influence in the decision-making processes of the church. By virtue of the limitations of their ministerial rank they are not qualified, according to COG polity, to be appointed or elected to most leadership positions in the church. While there have been repeated attempts to eliminate this barrier, to this point, all motions and votes have been lost after what have been long, heated, and often demeaning discussions of the role of women in church and ministry in the GC. These discussions normally center on whether or not allowing women to serve in leadership positions with the title OB is a violation of Scripture. Literalistic readings of selected texts in the Pauline corpus (but not all!) seldom take into consideration the texts which many interpreters, some within the COG, would see as providing warrant for full participation of women.[13] Beyond the fundamentalist hermeneutic evident in the discussions, other issues "beyond the text" are also apparent including political ideologies at work, lack of consideration for historical precedent, theological inconsistencies and, perhaps most importantly, an anthropology and view of sexuality that is inconsistent with a Wesleyan-Pentecostal hermeneutic.[14]

13. See Thomas, "Women, Pentecostals and the Bible," 41–56; "Biblical Reflections," 135–40. See also Alexander and Gause, *Women in Leadership*, 25–76.

14. While this study will not address all of these factors, it will illumine

Since the survey was conducted, the only notable changes with regard to the functional restrictions on women from full participation in the leadership of the organization were made in 2012 when the word "male" was deleted from qualifications for general, state, and regional standing boards and committees. This move did give women voice with regard to some functions in the denomination but, in fact, they are still barred from primary leadership positions of power and authority by virtue of continuing to be excluded from the ranks of the OB. In 2016, a recommendation that the General Council be open to all Ordained Ministers and Bishops aged twenty-five and older, a move that would have given both women and men OMs voice and vote in the powerful General Assembly agenda-setting body, was not passed.[15]

---

how this gestalt of influences has impacted Pentecostal women in ministry in the Church of God.

15. In summary, administrative posts/councils/committees still explicitly prohibited for women include: Ordained Bishop, International General Council, International Executive Committee, International Executive Council, ministerial trial boards, State/Regional Administrative Bishops, State/Regional Councils, and District Overseer. There are exceptional cases where women serve on national, territorial, and/or provincial councils, often due to an insufficient number of OBs in the area. In at least one district in California, a woman serves as District Overseer. Posts not specifically prohibited for women are: International General Assembly; standing boards and committees at general, state, and regional levels; local Church and Pastor's Council; and general, state, and local Women's Ministries Directors. The following posts do not specify gender, though they are normally filled by male ministers: International Council, State Youth and Discipleship Director, State Evangelism and Missions Director. In the past, when the State Youth and Discipleship Director's position was not a full-time (salaried) position, in some cases, women served. COG historian Roebuck assesses the situation in this way: "The primary office from which women are excluded is that of ordained bishop. All other exclusions relate to offices where the General Assembly Minutes state or the assumption is made that the officer must be an Ordained Bishop" (email correspondence with David G. Roebuck, January 31, 2018). Mireya Alvarez notes that there have been women serving as District Overseers and "educational positions generally reserved for male bishops" in Latin America (Alvarez, "Attitude is Everything," 98).

SHOULD WE CONDUCT SURVEY RESEARCH ON PENTECOSTAL WOMEN MINISTERS?

As noted earlier, research on the contemporary realities and factors affecting full equality for women in ministry was considered essential to better understanding and meaningful progress. Some may question, however, whether conducting survey research on Pentecostal women ministers will serve any useful purpose. In fact, a few women respondents expressed the sentiment that such research is unwelcome and spiritually detrimental. Although those expressing a negative attitude represented a miniscule number of women ministers, there are no doubt others—women and men—who question the authority and value of empirical research in the discussion or decision-making for issues of church polity or matters of faith. Why not simply decide all such issues based on scriptural teaching, the leadership of the Holy Spirit, or established church teaching?

Survey data, obviously, is not a substitute for scriptural teaching, the leadership of the Holy Spirit, or guidance from church teaching. Pentecostals, however, have a history of discerning and receiving such leadership, instruction, and guidance in the context of real life. Truthfully, all such understanding as arises from Scripture, the Spirit, or church teaching comes in some context and in the face of real needs and issues of faith and life. This survey research is not a substitute for those authorities but, rather, will hopefully provide a reality-based context in which to appropriate their guidance. Of course, survey data is descriptive, not prescriptive; that is, it gives a snapshot of the reality as it presently exists and cannot, in itself, prescribe how to respond to the reality. As none of us engages needs and concerns in a vacuum, the data examined in this report can help us to move beyond conjecture, speculation, and anecdotal limitations, and approach the questions surrounding the vocation of Pentecostal women ministers with the benefit of disciplined attention to their real experience and context.[16] If

16. Don S. Browning proposed the need for "descriptive theology within practical theology. See Browning, "Fundamental and Strategic Practical

this research report helps us have a more informed conversation and discern more faithful responses to God's call of women for ministry leadership, it will have achieved an important purpose.

HOW WAS THE SURVEY CONDUCTED?

Research data contained in this book was collected by administering a "Women in Ministry" (WIM) survey in 2012 to US Pentecostal women ministers in the COG. Pilot versions of the survey were sent to approximately twenty-five women ministers to test the validity and clarity of questions, with some modifications made based on feedback and analysis. A parallel WIM survey was also administered to 1,000 randomly selected US male OBs. The WIM survey consisted of forty-five questions, with different types of responses required of survey participants. At the time the survey was administered, there were 3,088 licensed women COG ministers in the United States. Of this population, the COG International Offices was able to provide email contact information for 2,379, or 77 percent, of female ministers who were all sent invitations and web links to the survey. Survey response rate was 30.5 percent of the female ministers contacted—which is typical of web-based survey research—and 23.5 percent of the total United States population of COG female ministers with 726 surveys completed. Methodologically, this was a "convenience sample" as survey participants were finally determined by email accessibility and respondent self-selection. The large number of respondents (726 of 3088) justifies high confidence that the sample is reflective of the views and experiences of the larger population of COG Pentecostal women ministers.[17]

Theology," 295–28; See also Bowers, "Practices in the Spirit," 252.

17. The sample utilized, as noted, was not random but determined by email accessibility. Emails were available for 77 percent of the entire population, however, and all 77 percent were emailed invitations to participate. If the sample were truly random, we could be 95 percent sure that answers would not vary more than 3.18 percent on any question for the larger population of COG women ministers. Indeed, some census-based research conducted in the COG has claimed high confidence and a small margin of error without randomly

Female respondents were from forty-five states and the District of Columbia with the largest concentration in the Southern states of Florida, Tennessee, North Carolina, Georgia, Virginia, Maryland, South Carolina, Alabama, Kentucky, and Mississippi. Respondents were diverse in ethnicity, age, and community profile. Comparison with the US COG women minister population reveals strong correspondence in age and ethnicity and, with other factors, is indicative of sample conclusions suggestive of the views, attitudes, and experiences of all US COG women ministers.[18]

For comparisons between ethnicities, Caucasian and African-American women are best represented in the sample, but such comparisons were kept to a minimum in this report.

Geographic Distribution of Female Respondents

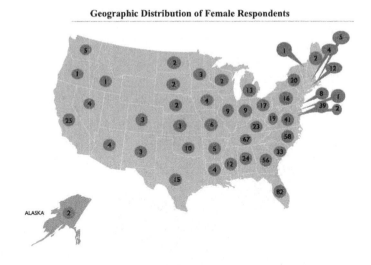

----

sampled respondents. In a small population (3088), random sampling is less important if the number of respondents is sufficient and varied.

18. See Appendix 2 for charts revealing the ethnic and age demographics for the US COG female ministry population at the time of this report.

Community Profile

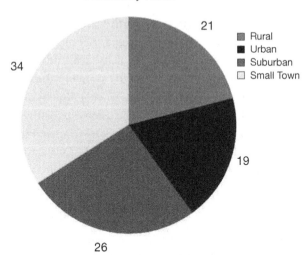

21
Rural
Urban
Suburban
Small Town
34
19
26

Age Range of Respondents

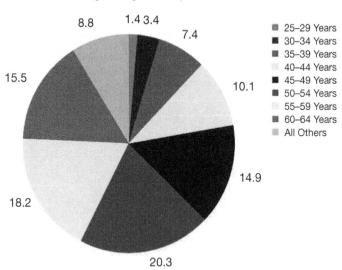

8.8 1.4 3.4
7.4
15.5
10.1
25–29 Years
30–34 Years
35–39 Years
40–44 Years
45–49 Years
50–54 Years
55–59 Years
60–64 Years
All Others
14.9
18.2
20.3

The response rate for the 1,000 randomly selected male OBs was much lower, with only 16 percent or 160 surveys completed. The ethnic profile for male respondents was similar to that of female respondents, with the exceptions that many more respondents were white (non-Hispanic) and significantly fewer were African-American. Age demographics for the two groups of respondents were also very similar, with most male and female respondents falling in the forty to sixty-five age range. More female than male respondents percentagewise were in the fifty-five-to-sixty-four age group. The type of community in which male respondents lived was virtually identical to those of female respondents.

As can be hypothesized in relation to women respondents, the OBs who completed the survey might be those with strong opinions for or against the full enfranchisement of women ministers. Initially, some responses on questions of women's leadership suggest the OB sample might be more progressive than the larger population of US OBs. This could also be indicated by the much larger percentage claiming to have participated in Pastoral Covenant Groups (PCGs) where they *may* have spent time with women pastors.[19] On balance, however, the views expressed by the respondent OBs on women ministers was not significantly different from those that prevailed in the COG GC debates of the GA. The sample of OBs—although randomly selected—was not large enough for a confidence interval or margin of error on responses any less than about 8 percent, meaning responses of the larger population could vary as much as 8 percent from the sample on any particular question. So, while the OB findings are "indicative" of the larger OB population, they are not conclusive of their views.[20]

19. Only about 17 percent of US COG pastors participated in such groups, but over 60 percent of the OB respondents claim to have been involved in a group. Other research findings indicate that such Pastoral Covenant Group participation contributes to more progressive views on various issues of ministry and mission.

20. As noted, a random sample of 1,000 OBs was selected and emailed an invitation to complete a similar survey to that completed by women ministers. Given a response rate of 16 percent, the margin of error or confidence interval is 7.66 percent with a 95 percent confidence level. Obviously, a larger sample

COG women ministers are compared to OBs on matters of compensation, advancement, and other questions in this report. An argument can be made that a more accurate comparison could be made between ordained women ministers and ordained male ministers because they are both of the same rank in the COG system. We believe that such a comparison would be more problematic because women cannot become an OB, while males normally progress upward to that level of ministry rank, with its expanded privileges and opportunities. This research, then, examines the *potential* for women with regard to leadership, affirmation and compensation. For the purposes of this study, understanding the potential or lack thereof for affirmation and fulfillment in ministry for women compared to men is better indicated by looking at OBs—who make up most US COG pastors and over 50 percent of all male ministers. Finally, given COG polity, comparing the views of the OBs to those of all women ministers makes sense because these men *are* the decision-makers or the potential change agents on questions related to women's leadership roles in congregations, states, and in the denomination.

HOW WAS THIS REPORT PREPARED?

Following the format used in *Portrait and Prospect: Church of God Pastors Face the 21st Century*,[21] an earlier empirical study of mostly male ministers, this book represents a preliminary report on key findings related to the experience of women in Pentecostal ministry leadership. Discussion of these findings is organized thematically. The two principal investigators, Kimberly Ervin Alexander and James P. Bowers, wrote the introductory and analytical chapters, with an outside observer's perspective provided by Cynthia Woolever. Each chapter also includes two responses by women ministers in order to create a dialogue about the challenges and opportunities for enhancing the prospects for future female minis-

would have been desirable, but the data collected is still considered indicative of the views and experiences of the larger population of OBs.

21. Bowers, *Portrait and Prospect*.

try leadership. Various appendices provide important supporting documents and data related to the conclusions narrated in this book.

WHO CAN BENEFIT FROM THIS BOOK?

A colleague referred to the study reported in this book as a form of "conflict action research." The purpose of such research is to address an immediate problem, usually in the social arena of life, with a view toward precipitating change. What does action research have to do with the question of who should read this book? The overarching goal of this research and this preliminary report is to give voice to the experience and views of Pentecostal women ministers serving in the COG. The polities of the COG and that of many other Pentecostal denominations restrict women ministers from having significant input in places of power, decision-making, and executive leadership. It is true that the International Church of the Foursquare Gospel and the Assemblies of God both have at least one woman at the executive level of their denominations, but the presence of women in such roles remains the exception and not the rule.[22] For instance, Ase-Miriam Smidsrad describes the situation in the Norwegian and Swedish movements, citing quantitative and qualitative research undertaken in both countries, with findings similar to those of the WIM.[23]

More extensive is the work of Gwendoline Malogne-Fer and Yannick Fer that examines the experiences of Pentecostal women in European, Middle Eastern, Central Africa, Australia, and Canada from an anthropological and sociological perspective. These case studies reveal the paradox of women who are "allowed significant roles in relating to God; but women are rarely, if ever allowed into the centers of power in Pentecostal churches."[24]

22. See Stephenson, "Prophesying Women," 410–26.

23. See Smidsrød, "For Such a Time," 200–20.

24. Bundy, Review of *Femmes et pentecôtismes*, 229. For the full study, see Malogne-Fer and Fer, *Femmes et pentecôtismes*. This paradox is also noted by Alminana and Olena in their assessment of the Assemblies of God in the

Given these realities, the purpose of this report is to allow Pentecostal women ministers—if only one group in one Pentecostal denomination—to finally speak for themselves. The hope is that when their voices are heard, their spiritual male leaders and ministry peers will listen, and change will come for women ministers for the good of the church, the advancement of the kingdom, and the glory of God. This book is for all those—be they women ministers, bishops, denominational leaders, or *even* a scholar or two—who are ready to end the silence of women and "hear what the Spirit is saying to the church."[25]

United States: "One might conclude that the phenomenon of women in leadership is a significant characteristic of Pentecostalism's ethos while at the same time it is only begrudgingly expressed in praxis." See English de Alminana and Olena, *Women*, 72.

25. Tomlinson, *Last Great Conflict*.

Chapter 2

What They Believe about Family

I was once told by a senior pastor that women could not bear the same heavy burdens that a man could. I asked him, had he ever taken care of four children alone?

DEBATE OVER THE IMPACT of political, sociological, economic and theological developments on the health of American families has figured prominently in contemporary public conversation. A "Family Values" movement has gained much attention in the news media, state and national political campaigns, and ecclesiastical policy and doctrinal discussions.[1] The inflammatory rhetoric of this movement sees divorce rates, single parenting, civil homosexual unions, increasing alternative family structures, and equal rights for women as a sinister attack on the "American family." A moral and theological orthodoxy dividing line has been drawn by "Family Values" activists between those who hold a "biblical view"

1. For instance, the COG (Cleveland, TN) General Assembly has now passed three resolutions (1976, 2004, and 2012) specifically expressing affirmation of traditional family values. These resolutions express concern for rising divorce rates, same-sex marriage unions, disappearance of the "nuclear family," and what is viewed as an associated movement away from the denomination's faith confession among children and youth.

and are "conservative" and those who are seen as having embraced an immoral, theologically compromised, and non-biblical view of the family and are "liberal."

In this research on gender and ministry in the COG, we wanted to know what influence, if any, the "Family Values" agenda has exerted on how the denomination has formulated its polity and theology on the role of women in ministry leadership. Some of the questions needing answers include the following:

- Where do COG women in ministry fall on the political spectrum? How does their political orientation compare to COG male OBs?

- Do COG women ministers desire full participation in denominational-level decision-making, opportunity to serve as OBs, and appointment to traditionally male ecclesiastical leadership roles because they embrace a secular feminist ideology?

- What role, if any, does the embrace of a conservative "Family Values" agenda have on how women and men ministers understand the role of women in ministry?

- What other factors influence how women and men ministers understand the role of women in ministry leadership in the COG?

Official and informal discussions of the role and authority of women in ministry in the COG have inevitably lead to consideration of questions about the "biblical order" of family life and the home. Specifically, proposed changes in COG polity that would expand the boundaries of ministerial authority and functioning for women are frequently interpreted as overt or, at least, implicit threats to what many understand as "traditional family values." Family structure, especially as it relates to the roles of wives and husbands, is assumed to be paradigmatic for gender roles in the church. Consequently, many who resist the fuller empowerment of women for ministerial leadership advanced through recently proposed COG polity changes do so because they believe such moves will work backward to undermine what they see as biblically sanctioned male leadership and a spiritual patriarchy in the home.[2] Belief that a liberal feminist agenda contrary to biblical teaching motivates the desire of women ministers for increased ministerial authority and recognition apparently leads many male ministers—who control denominational polity decisions and, therefore, any official change in the status of women ministers—to oppose the full empowerment of women.[3] Given the assumption that Scripture supports a patriarchal family structure with women subordinated to men, male ministers interpret full equality for women in ministry as undermining biblical authority. Therefore, what women want—in the eyes of many of their male ministerial peers—is to "usurp" authority and power as ministers who will dilute scriptural authority, undermine family order, and lead to a moral "slippery slope" in relation to family and other social culture war issues.[4] Of course, women have not had the opportunity to

2. Belief in patriarchal male spiritual leadership as essential to family order and spirituality is readily visible in the remarks of COG General Council members addressing measures related to women in ministry. P. Douglas Small, COG International Prayer Ministry Liaison, regularly publishes blog posts asserting the primacy of male leadership in the home and has spoken against granting women equal status with male ministers. Insightfully, Small's assumptions about the importance of male spiritual leadership in the home are in direct conflict with the historical reality of female spiritual leadership evident in many Pentecostal families. See the Project Pray website "Mission Statement and Core Values," where article 7 states: "Finally, that fathers are critical not only to the family, but to the nation as spiritual leaders; and that when nations err, it is the turning of the hearts of fathers that most quickly averts judgment. Godly fathers are irreplaceable in the divine design."

3. Smidsrød cites a debate in Norwegian Christian news publications, covered in issues over the course of the year 2014. One pastor, Kent Andersen, is quoted as saying, "One wants to lower the standard to make it look better on paper . . . my impression is that many women leaders take up the gender card in order to explain the opposition" (Smidsrød, "For Such a Time," 208).

4. The traditional interpretation of 1 Timothy 2:12—"But I suffer not a woman to teach, nor to usurp authority over the man, but to be in silence"—among those opposed to full empowerment of women in ministry—is that this text prohibits women from having specific administrative oversight of male ministers and members. Although this is a contradictory position to the established affirmation of women serving as Pentecostal pastors, any steps to

speak for themselves in discussions at the state or denominational levels. To date, what women actually believe about the family and its relationship to questions of gender and ministry is merely a matter of speculation.

WHAT WOMEN BELIEVE ABOUT FAMILY

Before addressing what the WIM survey reveals about what women want in church and family roles, it is helpful to consider how women ministers responded to questions concerning their beliefs in this arena. We need to know what women believe about family relationships, the biblical role of women in church leadership, and whether they are viewing these concerns through a liberal political or feminist lens. Additionally, it will be insightful to know how the beliefs of the women ministers surveyed compare with those of male ministers surveyed who hold the rank of OB in the COG. Fortunately, our survey data provided answers in both areas.

MYTHBUSTER:

Equality for women ministers is motivated by a liberal political agenda.

Both women and men who express support for equality in ministry self-identify as politically conservative.

Political Orientation

Women ministers asked to characterize their political orientation in the WIM survey with choices between conservative, liberal, moderate, or other strongly identified with conservatism. More than three-fourths of all women described themselves as "Conservative." Not surprisingly, white women were most conservative (86 percent), with Hispanic women close behind (70 percent).

---

recognize women as Ordained Bishops in the COG or to further elevate them in leadership is interpreted as "usurpation"—wrongful seizure of authority or privilege—on the part of women.

African-American and Caribbean women were less conservative (both 51 percent) and, consequently, more "Moderate" and "Liberal" in their political views, but mostly "Moderate" (38 percent and 42 percent, respectively). While differences in ethnicity reflected some significant variation among women, COG women ministers are still predominantly politically "Conservative."

Political Orientation of Female Respondents

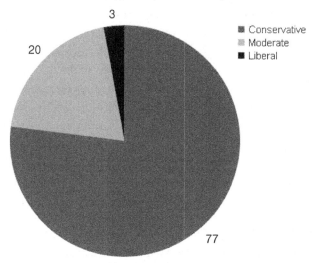

Male OBs surveyed on their political views were also predominantly "Conservative." While insufficient diversity was present in the male survey for conclusive judgments about ethnic differences, the same pattern of white and Hispanic strong "Conservative" identification was evident. The important observation for the purpose of this research is the essentially identical political profile of male respondents to that of women ministerial respondents. There is no reason, given the findings on the political orientation of male OBs and women ministers, to consider women ministers' pursuit of full empowerment for ministry leadership to be the result of different—certainly not liberal—political leanings from their male counterparts. Opponents of equal ministerial authority and responsibility between women and men ministers in the COG have no empirical or reality-based data for arguing such equality represents the growing influence of liberal political thinking among women, men, or minorities. Indeed, this study's findings specifically repudiate that idea.

Family Values

Another frequently invoked apologetic for maintaining the status quo of subordinate ministerial authority for women in relation to men concerns the conviction that the undermining of biblical or at least traditional "family values" will result from any change. The "Family Values" argument links discussions of the full equality of women ministers to the "Culture Wars" phenomenon in the United States and suggests women seek to undermine healthy, biblically understood family life. Do the views of women ministers on family life and the roles of women and men in the home support this fear? Are women ministers pursuing fuller ministerial empowerment in order to flip the traditional view of family on its head, or even to tilt the order of the home for their greater influence?

As it turns out, women ministers hold rather conservative or traditional views on family roles. The majority of women (55 percent) agreed: "men are the scripturally designated priests of the home." While Caribbean (64 percent) and African-American (57 percent) women were most affirming of male spiritual leadership in the home, there were no appreciable differences based on ethnicity. Additionally, a significant minority of all female ministers (17 percent) said "women have voice with men making the final decisions" in the home, tantamount to a male-dominant perspective on the home. Notably, more than a quarter of women surveyed (28 percent) believe that "Women and men share equal spiritual responsibility and leadership in the home." On balance, however, nearly three-fourths of female ministers (72 percent) support the priority of male spiritual- and decision-making leadership and, therefore, a rather traditional view of family roles.

MYTHBUSTER:

Women seeking equality as ministers undermine marriage and family.

Most women ministers actually hold traditional family views and are supported by spouses and family members in ministerial vocation.

Male OBs surveyed responded with very similar views to those of female ministers. The largest number affirmed men as "the scripturally designated priests of the home," and a smaller number (15 percent) held the view that "women have voice with men making the final decisions." Further paralleling the responses of female ministers, one-quarter (24 percent) believe men and women "share equal spiritual responsibility and leadership in the home."

Role of Women and Men in the Home

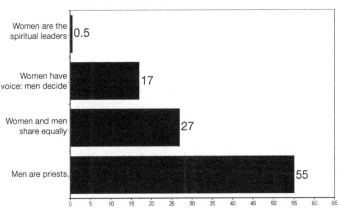

Thus, the views of women and men on their respective roles in the home are strikingly compatible, invalidating any claim that women are seeking fuller ministerial empowerment as part of a move away from any correctly or incorrectly assumed biblical justification for male dominance in family life or in order to oppose family values.

Church Order

Despite the virtually parallel views of women and men ministers on "family values" as it relates to husband/wife roles, male respondents who believe there are reasons other than those found in Scripture for women not serving in traditionally male roles. These respondents identified violation of "God-ordained order for the home" as the main reason (61 percent). Many also opposed full ministerial equality for women because it "violates God-ordained order for society" (53 percent). Interestingly, male and female ministers surveyed strongly agreed that "women should serve in civic or government leadership" (90 percent and 97 percent, respectively). While most female ministers (84 percent) believe "women and men have full and equal authority in the church," of those citing reasons other than Scripture for restricting the role of women, 59 percent identified "difficulty some men have with women in leadership" as the main reason. Other reasons women gave outside of Scripture for restrictions on their ministry leadership included lack of support from denominational leaders (46 percent) and lack of support from congregations (35 percent).[5]

CONCLUSION

Survey findings reviewed in this chapter reveal important insights into what women want in regard to the family values agenda and its relationship to their ministry functioning. Given the parallel conservative political orientation of women and men ministers in the COG, it isn't credible to suggest that fuller empowerment of women in ministry is motivated by a liberal political or secular feminist agenda. Additionally, the support of male spiritual leadership in the home by women in agreement with their male counterparts invalidates any suggestion that women ministers are seeking

---

5. Smidsrød notes that, in interviews of Swedish Pentecostal women ministers conducted by Jenny Bergh and Anethe Carlson in 2013, difficulties that they faced in ministry were related to their male colleagues. See Smidsrød, "For Such a Time," 204.

to undermine traditional "family values" as they are presently understood in the United States. What women want in pursuing full recognition of their ministry calling and gifts is not necessarily a reordering of family roles.

Interestingly, despite the parallel political orientations and family leadership understandings between women and men ministers, male OB survey respondents believe allowing women full access to ministerial leadership roles traditionally reserved for men "violates God-ordained order for the home" (61 percent). Male OBs also believe such empowerment for women "violates God-ordained order for society" (53 percent) even though, in agreement with women, these same men affirmed "women should serve in civic or government leadership" (90 percent). Women admittedly see male ministerial resistance to their empowerment for ministry as the major obstacle (59 percent) even though they overwhelmingly believe that "women and men have full and equal authority in the church" (84 percent). What women ministers want is not to overturn the conservative "family values" vision of home life, but the affirmation of their ministerial calling and gifts. What they want and need is a renewed vision of the relationship between domestic roles in the home and gendered ministry in the church that recognizes the distinction between God's call and gifts in these different spheres.

A RESPONSE: REV. MIREYA ALVAREZ, BA, MA, DMin

Vice-President for Academic Affairs, Asian Seminary of Christian Ministries

The data gathered by Alexander and Bowers reflects the differing perspectives over women's roles in society, home, and the church. On one hand, more than 90 percent of both male and female ministers agreed "women should serve in civic or government leadership," meaning they endorse a public role for women. However, in relation to a church office, a good number of male ministers still link what is considered the biblical family order to what should also occur in the church. The conclusion that women in church must be subject to male authority inevitably limits or restricts any spiritual contribution that the Holy Spirit places upon women who normally comprise more than 50 percent of church membership.

However, current examples of COG Latina ministers have challenged the traditional framework in which many North American churches still operate. Several churches in Latin America have opened the way for women to exercise governing authority. For example, in the city of Tegucigalpa, Honduras, a female minister is a district overseer and a woman minister is a regional director in the Board of Education, positions previously reserved for male bishops. A female minister who reports more than 3,000 members is described as a woman who has broken paradigms in a church society generally led by men.

In an article entitled "The View from the Pulpit," female clergy expressed the unique challenges they faced and shared about their common obstacles: exclusion from colleagues, unsupportive seminary professors, criticism due to their leadership style, gender discrimination, and perceptions of being not feminine enough or not forceful enough.[6]

My ministerial experience in the Church of God goes back at least thirty years. I have been able to engage in a variety of ministry opportunities in Latin America, Asia, and US Hispanic churches. I never doubted His calling upon my life based upon Joel 2:28: "I will pour out my Spirit on all people. Your sons and daughters will prophesy." However, I have also lamented the controversies in Pentecostal circles about the restriction of women in ministry.

What women ministers want is to be defenders of the Gospel, bearers of the gifts of the Spirit, and affirmed as created in God's image (Gen 1:27).

6. Spencer, "View from the Pulpit," https://www.cbeinternational.org/resources/article/mutuality/view-pulpit.

A RESPONSE: REV. DR. MARY RUTH (MORRIS) STONE, BA, MS, MCM, EDD

Retired; former International Coordinator of Women's Ministries, Church of God and Director of Faculty Development, Lee University

On a purely personal level, I cannot imagine secular culture dictating my view of gender equality in ministry and/or my view of "order" in the marriage relationship. I cannot imagine fear of gender equality in ministry somehow negatively affecting relationships with the males in my family of origin and/or my marriage. It was, after all, my father first and then my husband who instilled in me the concept of gender equality within the home as well as the church. Yet both my father and my husband filled the biblical role of headship, and both my mother and I were/are submissive to them.

Chapter 2 elicited for me the Old Testament story of Deborah and the military man Barak. The writer of chapters 4 and 5 of the book of Judges did not find it somehow wrong or dangerous to write and sing about Deborah, a woman who was called in the same sentence "a prophetess, the wife of Lapidoth . . . judging Israel" (Judg 4:4, NKJV). Her three roles—prophetess, wife, and judge—were neither mutually exclusive nor each destructive of the others. It was God, not culture, who placed her in those roles, who gave her influence over Barak, and who accompanied her to war even as she accompanied Barak.

In the Deborah narrative, we are given a glimpse of a military victory led by a male and female team, Barak and Deborah. In celebration of victory, Deborah and Barak sang a song called "Bless the Lord" after the defeat of King Jabin and Sisera. In that song of Deborah's victory as a warrior, a traditionally male role, she is described like this: "I, Deborah, arose, arose a mother in Israel" (Judg 5:7, NKJV). The male role of warrior and the female role of mother were not considered mutually exclusive. Neither were the roles destructive one of the other.

The story of Deborah is a metaphor for the kind of leadership today's women in ministry desire and deserve if and when God calls them to it, as he did the prophetess, wife, judge, warrior, and mother of Judges 4 and 5.

Chapter 3

How Power and Leadership Function

*I have a young daughter who is contemplating the call of God
on her own life. I have not tried to push this on her, because
I know that it must be God calling her for her to stand. I also
know that, as a woman minister, I am paving the road for
other young women who receive that call from God. I would
like to see her and others be accepted and receive support for
that calling. I know that she will be a leader in this world and I
hope that she will be a leader in the Church of God.*

GIVEN THE RESPONSIBILITIES AND privileges invested in the rank
of OB, it is clear that power in the COG rests, for the most part,
with those obtaining to and holding that credential. In this ongoing debate within the denomination, what has been at issue for
most is an understanding of New Testament texts that prescribe
qualifications for the office of "bishop." Discussions on the floor of
the GC have revealed a variety of hermeneutical models within the
denomination, all of which claim a high view of Scripture and see
it as authoritative. In general, university trained biblical scholars
have called for an interpretation that takes into consideration the
diversity of the whole of scriptural witness; others have expressed

interpretations with appeal to the larger Christian and Pentecostal tradition; still others have voiced literalistic interpretations focusing on Pauline texts that would, if taken at face value, seem to exclude women from leadership positions.[1]

In 2010, Britt Peavy (OB), a senior pastor from Douglas, Georgia, was quoted in *The Christian Century* as expressing this point of view: "This has nothing to do with women not being smart enough or good enough or qualified enough." He continued, "The issue is, did God know what he was talking about? And whether we like it or don't like it . . . if our rules, our standard, is biblical text, then we have to be faithful to the biblical text even in contemporary society that sees it as bigoted or old-fashioned."[2]

Given the COG's broad understanding of the term "bishop," this discussion does not simply have a bearing on those in top leadership within the COG hierarchy, but also upon the advancement of women pastors to larger congregations, their acceptance as pastors of congregations, their access to leadership at the district level, and therefore compensation and ability to serve in full-time ministry, concerns discussed elsewhere in this volume.

In order to assess what COG women ministers want with regard to power and leadership roles, it is necessary to first understand how *they* interpret these texts and qualifications.

WHAT DO COG WOMEN MINISTERS BELIEVE ABOUT THEIR ROLES?

Titles and Function

Several survey questions are pertinent to this discussion and reveal that a large majority of women completing the survey are in

---

1. In 2006, the COG Doctrine and Polity Commission solicited position papers on the issue of women's ordination from COG scholars. Four of these papers were printed and distributed to OBs and published on the COG website in preparation for the General Assembly. They are no longer available online.

2. "Church of God," para. 5.

agreement that they should be granted both the privileges and responsibilities associated with the rank of OB.

MYTHBUSTER:

A radical feminist agenda is being pushed by a few women.

Women overwhelmingly believe they are qualified and within scriptural boundaries to serve as OBs and at the highest levels of ministry leadership.

When directly asked if they believe that women ministers should be recognized as "Ordained Bishops" in the COG, nearly three-fourths (74 percent) of females surveyed affirmed this belief with only one-fourth (26 percent) answering "no." There is little variation on this item among ethnicities with one exception. Among the African-Americans answering this question, 67 percent said "yes"; of the Caribbean respondents, 70 percent answered in the affirmative, while 74 percent of white respondents did so. The exceptions are the Hispanic respondents, of whom 96 percent responded "yes."[3]

3. Given the lower representation of Caribbean and Hispanic women, the significance of their responses in comparison to white and African-American women should not be the basis of any certain conclusions about ethnic attitudes. One cannot ignore that, of those Hispanic women who were survey respondents, a very high percentage affirmed the full empowerment of women ministers as OBs, especially when one remembers that Hispanic women have been leading the charge for equality in US COG GA deliberations. There is no doubt, however, that the large percentage of women of all ethnicities who responded affirmatively indicates a strong desire to see women recognized as OBs.

Should women be recognized as
"Ordained Bishops"?

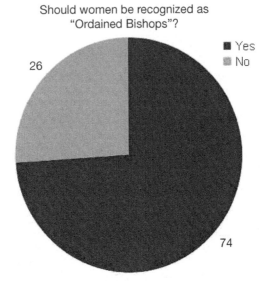

When this pool is broken down based on educational demographics, the trends are striking. In general, the more educated the woman minister, the more likely she is to affirm her qualification to hold the OB credential. There is a steady increase in affirmative answers based on educational level, beginning with those obtaining high school diplomas or GED certificates (62 percent), to some college (73 percent), to bachelor's degrees (73 percent), to master's degrees (80 percent) and lastly, to the doctoral level (83 percent). While a majority of women at all levels affirm the validity of female OBs, it is clear that education enables women to be even more confident of this belief.

The responses of male ministers follow similar patterns on the whole, but with lower rates of affirmation. A small majority of male ministers (54 percent) affirmed that women should be recognized as OBs. An even lower majority of white male ministers (52 percent) answered "yes," while 73 percent of Hispanic males did so.

The educational variable is even more significant. Only 13 percent of male ministers who have no college education believe women should serve as OBs. However, that statistic jumps considerably with only some college experience, to 58 percent. Those completing higher education degrees maintain a belief that women should serve as OBs (bachelor's degree, 53 percent; master's degree 65 percent; doctorate, 59 percent).

> *To me, I am sixty-eight years old, and it doesn't make a lot of difference. But to the younger generation, I would love to see them be able to move forward.*
> *What's mostly at stake is the fullness of God's blessing on the denomination. Somewhere out there are Deborahs and Esthers whom God could use to save our people from future destruction. Isn't the completed image of God both male and female? Without it, whether in the home or denomination, we are incomplete. Didn't Paul say to Timothy, "if any man [any person, whosoever] aspires to the office of overseer, it is a fine work he desires to do"?*

As stated earlier, the ambivalence with regard to women owning the title OB seems to be related to biblical interpretation. When asked if they believe Scripture teaches against women serving as "Ordained Bishops," an even higher percentage of women responded "no" (80 percent).[4] In comments, women cite biblical examples of leadership such as Deborah, Abigail, and Esther.[5]

---

4. A similar increase is noted among male ministers, where 56 percent respond that Scripture does not teach that women cannot serve as bishops.

5. Smidsrød cites qualitative research conducted for a 2007 MA thesis. In this research conducted by Bjørg Marie Stubberud Vrabel, interviews with male and female ministers revealed this: "Both sides argued from the Bible, but those in favour of female elders also argued from the roots and and history of the NPM [Norwegian Pentecostal Movement]" (Vrabel, "Kvinnelige eldste og forstandere," 206).

Does Scripture teach against women
serving as "Ordained Bishops"?

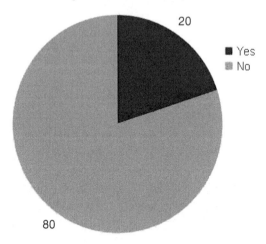

20

■ Yes
▓ No

80

When the questions refer to *functional* roles and responsibilities designated for OBs, the responses among female respondents are even more overwhelmingly affirming. This suggests that the use of the biblical term "bishop" may be somewhat problematic for COG adherents who cherish biblical authority. This is evidenced, first, in that women clearly believe that they are qualified to vote in the GC "currently composed of only male 'Ordained Bishops.'" Nearly 90 percent of those surveyed answered "yes," while only 54 percent of men respondents held the same view. Interestingly, white women were slightly less affirming (87 percent); African-American women overwhelmingly affirm their ability to perform this function (99 percent). Again, there is a steady increase of confidence with educational levels among female respondents (from 86 percent to 97 percent).[6]

Second, women are confident that their gender should not bar them from leading the church at the state and denominational levels (87 percent), while men are only slightly convinced of the

6. For male respondents, educational levels follow the same patterns as in earlier questions, with a significant jump from 13 percent for those with high school/GED education to 55 percent of those with some college education.

same (51 percent). Once again, white respondents, both male and female, were somewhat less confident than the average among their peers. African-American and Hispanic women are the most convinced (95 percent and 94 percent respectively). Hispanic men (at 82 percent) fall only slightly below the average for their female peers in ministry. Statistical breakdowns along educational levels followed a nearly identical pattern as in previous questions.

Third, as one might expect, when asked about the general capability of women to serve in church leadership roles normally open only to men, women affirm their capability with a resounding 93 percent. As one respondent writes, "I have many years of experience in administrative work. I have no doubt that I could effectively serve in an administrative capacity. If I could do so with my limited education, I know there are other women out there who could do so."

Interestingly, there is strong affirmation of women's capabilities as leaders among males. While only 54 percent believe women are qualified to vote in the GC and just 51 percent believe gender should not bar women from denominational leadership, confidence in women's *capabilities* are not in question for nearly 80 percent of male minister respondents. This disparity points to the highly likely explanation that, for male ministers, the restrictions placed on women ministers are not a result of their lack of gifts or abilities; instead, they are determined by a particular reading of Scripture and a particular interpretation of the word "bishop": the office of bishop is an office of authority and power; women are to be restricted from having authority and therefore institutional power.

A final question should be considered when attempting to understand what is believed about women in leadership roles within the COG. The survey asked the question, "Do you believe that Scripture teaches against women serving as senior pastors?" It should be reiterated here that the COG does not now and has never held the view that women should not or could not serve in pastoral roles over congregations. The irony of this dualistic position that allows women to "oversee" a local congregation, but not to "oversee" other ministers or multiple congregations, has not been lost on scholars.[7]

The survey reveals that 92 percent of women surveyed believe that women are permitted by Scripture to lead congregations; 71 percent of men held the same view. While this is a large majority of the male OBs surveyed, it is noteworthy that nearly 30 percent of them believe that Scripture forbids women from holding senior pastoral roles over congregations, a position never upheld by the COG.

The only significant finding with regard to ethnicity was that both Hispanic women and men responded with less affirmation of this role. Hispanic women responded with slightly less affirmation (89 percent), while African-American women were most likely to affirm that Scripture permits women to serve as senior pastors (96 percent). Hispanic men were less likely than their white male peers to support this view (64 percent and 70 percent respectively). The implication of this finding with regard to ethnicity may indicate that Hispanic Pentecostals have some degree of unease with regard to women in roles of what may be perceived as *spiritual* leadership versus *administrative* function.

Based on these findings about beliefs with regard to the title and function of OBs in the COG, it is difficult not to come to the conclusion that the change in nomenclature for the highest ranking credential from OM to OB in effect reinforced the "stained glass ceiling" for women and the patriarchal view of the episcopate. The data reinforces the earlier stated thesis that hermeneutical issues are primary, but also suggests that other factors are at work in determining what is believed about the qualifications of women for leadership.

Other Beliefs

In order to ascertain what else may be at work in determining what beliefs help to undergird these barriers to power, respondents were

7. See Alexander and Gause, *Women in Leadership*. See also Appendix 1.

surveyed regarding what they "believe" are the reasons that women are restricted from positions of leadership in the COG. Of the women who responded, 85 percent stated that they believed there were no other such reasons. A follow-up question asked those who believed there were other reasons to select from a pool of possible "reasons," selecting all that applied. There were 279 respondents. The answers given by women are revealing, especially when compared to their male counterparts.[8]

Other reasons that could be cited for women
not serving as leaders

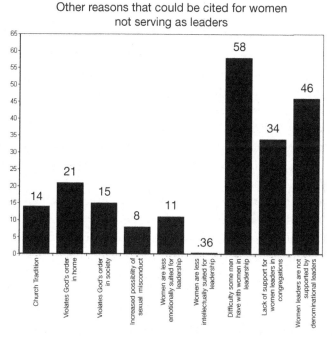

For these women, the number one "other reason" cited was "difficulty some men have with women in leadership" (58 percent). The reason ranked second was "no support from denominational leaders" (46 percent). Those with doctoral degrees were more likely to select this as the main reason, indicating an awareness

8. It is important to note the wording of this follow-up question: "If there are other reasons [other than scriptural ones] why women should not serve in ministry or leadership roles traditionally held by men, which of the following reasons would you give?"

of, or skepticism about, a lack of support at the leadership level of the COG. The third reason most often cited was "lack of support in congregations" (34 percent). Obviously, a significant number of women sense that their gender is an obstacle to their ability to minister effectively given the lack of support by male leadership, as well as by congregations. Lamenting this systemic problem, one woman commented, "As a licensed therapist, I do understand that men and women tend to think about the world differently. However, that difference should be considered an enrichment, not an inferiority issue." In other words, gender differences should be recognized as valuable for the work of ministry. Another female minister speaks of the diversity in theological terms: "This diversity of shared responsibility and equal rights would also reflect the Trinity's work of being distinct entities, yet existing in a united relationship." In other words, essential differences do not necessitate a hierarchical structure. Whether one sees differences as complementary and cause for inclusion and celebration, or as implying inferiority and justification for subordination or, worse, domination, is a matter of the intentions, desires, and preferences of the interpreter. Others lamented that the effectiveness of the COG is diminished by its lack of support of women ministers; in particular, one woman noted that it places the church in a "precarious position," like a person attempting to stand on one leg.

Only 21 percent cited the belief that it "violates the God-given order for the home."[9] What is most revealing here is that the top three reasons cited by women ministers in the COG all have to do with the attitudes and support, or lack thereof, of others, notably men.

Not surprisingly, the 70 percent of the men who believe there are other reasons that women should not serve in positions of leadership ranked those reasons quite differently than their female colleagues in ministry. The two top reasons cited by men, again, are connected to a particular biblical interpretation. The most often cited reason was that to do so "violates the God-ordained order

9. The wording of this reason does not make it clear whether this is the view of the women responding or of what others in positions of power believe.

for the home" (60 percent). The next most cited is similar: to allow women to lead "violates the God-ordained order for society" (51 percent). The vast majority of these respondents were white. More overtly culturally conditioned views also come to bear on this question of "other reasons." Nearly one-third of those responding see "the problem some men have with women" to be significant, and one-third viewed women as "less emotionally suited." Again, these views were more prominent among white males.

A reason often cited in public discourse and alluded to in GC discussions of the issue of full participation of women (whether at the denominational or local church leadership levels) is the likelihood of an increased possibility of sexual misconduct between men and women serving together. It was expected that this would be a widely held view. However, only 14 percent of males cited this as a reason and, interestingly, all of those were white. Fewer than 10 percent of women saw this as a real danger; that percentage was slightly higher among women with only a high school diploma or GED. However, at least two women made comments about their vulnerability to sexual harassment, indicating that women ministers are "targets," as one said, for both "married and unmarried men."

MYTHBUSTER:

Women and men working together in leadership will lead to sexual misconduct.

Only 14 percent of male ministers and fewer than 10 percent of female ministers cite the increased potential for sexual misconduct as problematic.

Clearly the potential for sexual misconduct is a minority view, but regularly functions as an emotionally charged and anxiety-producing argument in speeches and discussions. That this issue is so often raised in GC discussions or even less formal settings is revealing. Ministers' wives fearing their husbands being placed in potentially threatening situations sometimes make this argument.

Additionally, "slippery slope" arguments are made by those who fear full participation of women is a first step in a move toward liberalism that will end in ordination of homosexuals.

WHAT CONCLUSIONS MAY BE DRAWN?

First, it is very clear that women ministers in the COG believe they should be allowed to function as bishops in the church. It is their conclusion that, according to Scripture, they are not prohibited from doing so. Second, it is even clearer that they believe that they have the capability to function as bishops with regard to decision-making, administration, and leadership. Third, women are quite aware that the impediments to their being able to serve in this capacity are the lack of support of male ministers, in general, and denominational leaders, in particular. Fourth, women employ a different hermeneutic with regard to reconciling the texts often cited by their male counterparts in order to exclude women from full participation. Women are informed by a narrative reading of the text and by one more consistent with a relational theology. Additionally, women ministers, while holding to a conservative view of order in the home, are likely to discern the difference in the functions of the two arenas of church and home. Finally, for neither female or male ministers is the likelihood of sexual impropriety between male and female ministers working together a significant reason for prohibition of women's full participation. While the increased likelihood of sexual misconduct is often cited as a significant risk in debates about the full empowerment of women, there is no evidence that it is understood to be so among survey respondents and, likely, not viewed as such by most women and men COG ministers.

A RESPONSE: REV. EMILY BROWN STONE, MDɪᴠ, MA, PʜD, LMFT

Assoc. Prof., Pfeiffer University

"It's not personal": a statement I have heard more than once when dialoguing about the role of women in the church. It is usually made by some well-intentioned white male attempting to assuage the pain inflicted when sharing a stance against women in leadership. It's not personal—but it most certainly is.

People of color have long been forced to practice a rich, narrative, relational hermeneutical reading of scripture due to their history of abuse and being the target of prejudice. Their God seems bigger than boxes or misuses of scriptures that tell slaves to return to their master. Their God seems to refuse to stay within the boundaries of white folk. They have been reading God's word in context for a long time.

White privilege has its liabilities. Our version of God is at times very small. Our bibles and its characters—or our limited understanding of them—are flat. We certainly do see through a dark glass dimly. It is grimy with our fingerprints, as we have put our hands all over the text—grabbing it and begging it to stay within the boundaries of our safe, white, often southern, world.

If this is true for whites, it is even truer for white men. We are talking about power here. Leadership, sure, but *power*. It is not merely intoxicating. When slipping away, it is the root of terror. People do and say crazy things when they are afraid. Nothing brings more fear than change, especially change that threatens loss of power (and control). As a licensed marriage and family therapist, I have seen sad and frightening attempts to regain a sense of power. Unfortunately, it is the most insecure and power*less* that seek to obtain or retain that which they feel makes up for their impotence.

As a fifth-generation COG member, a woman, and a minister highly invested in (read: sold out to) the furthering of God's kingdom, let me be very clear. I am disillusioned and apathetic to this cause. From where I stand working out in the world, befriending non-Christians and enjoying a history of living abroad, this is a non-issue. It is irrelevant, as is my denomination much of the time. I am still in the Church of God because it is home. As my husband, Jonathan Stone, a COG OB, has stated: "It will be my home until my spiritual fathers and mothers ask me to leave. I do not plan on backing out the back door quietly as so many of my brothers and sisters have." I am here. I adhere to the majority of its theology. I want my children raised in my local church. It is our home.

Still, I have left the dialoguing around this issue within the confines of my denomination. I am done. As blogger Sarah Bessey once wrote: "I am done fighting for a seat at the table. The one filled with white men, all reading the same books, spouting the same talking points, quoting each other back and forth. . . . Me? I am simply getting on with the business of the kingdom."[10]

A RESPONSE: REVEREND PAULETTE DAVIS, BA, MS, MS.

Clinical Mental Health Counseling, Nationally Certified Counselor (NBCC), Hospice Chaplain, Mobile, AL

As a second generation Church of God member, I was ardently COG from "shoe to hat." My life centered on the church: YPE (Young People's Endeavor), youth camp, camp meeting, district fellowship meeting, Teen Day, Saturday night singings and YWEA (Youth World Evangelism Appeal). I read the *Evangel* and *The Lighted Pathway*, used the *Pilot* for YPE programs, and poured over the monthly statistics in the *Alabama Echo*. I graduated from Lee College having never missed a convocation service, being a member of Pioneers for Christ, and revering all my Bible professors.

The one thing that I could not find within my church was a way to answer the calling that I recognized even before I entered my teen years. When I would summon my courage to talk to my pastor or Sunday School teacher or the most recent evangelist, I was heartily welcomed and quickly assured that God was calling

10. Bessey, "In Which I Am Done Fighting," paras. 1–3.

me to marry a preacher, using my talents as a minister's wife. My life in ministry was defined solely as a helpmate with no recognition that I had a personal call to minister.

After two college degrees and a firmly established teaching career had begun, I went to the State Overseer (now, AB) and poured out my heart for God, expressing as I had never before my desire to be in the ministry as a recognized, credentialed minister. He listened seemingly attentively, then, chose his words very carefully: "You need to continue serving God as He has truly called you . . . in the local church as a servant. You do not need credentials and you cannot be set forth in the ministry."

I decided not to accept the Overseer's answer, moved to another state, and was credentialed in the Church of God. Now I question why I did so. Other than the authority to perform marriages and to get me into hospital ICU units, my credentials are a piece of paper complete with a reporting requirement, but with little support, less recognition, and no chance of advancement. I love the Church of God. I have given my life in ministry while working a secular job, which happens to be one of my greatest ministry areas. I have, for most of my credentialed ministry, not received financial support from church ministry. My teaching career has made my ministry in the congregation possible.

As a bi-vocational minister, I am unable to attend any state ministerial meetings or other daytime activities. Financially, the GA is beyond my budget, but more than that, why should I attend? While I enjoy the worship services, the only other thing to be done as a woman minister is to rubberstamp the decisions made by the male OBs. The real business of discussing church issues, polity, and vision are closed to women ministers, and we are left seated with the laity, powerless to make a statement even when our ministry future and our fate within the COG are being debated, decided, and dismissed.

So, it is what it is. I have a ministry, rich and full. During my ministry, I have never had any contact from or with any of my State ABs. On the rare occasions that I have contacted the AB's office, the secretary would call me back with an answer. Of course, there have been seminars and conferences on women in ministry, but these never address the real issues—full recognition and the validity of our ministries and the full acceptance of our callings, which means full participation and involvement in all areas of ministry—administrative, pastoral, evangelistic, teaching, and even full ordination.

I have been and will continue to be a minister in the COG. I will support and love my church; and yet, I will agonize over the ministerial potential we continue to lose as we refuse to fully recognize, accept, and welcome women—called of God, anointed by God, wanted by God, and used by God, but in reality, unwelcomed within the hierarchy and full ministry of the COG. Will and should our young women answer the call of God within our church?

Chapter 4

Are Women Flourishing as Ministers?

God had been dealing with me for quite some time.
Being involved in church ministry for most of my life, I knew
the obstacles I would face as a woman in ministry. So, it was
with much prayer and hesitation that I went to my pastor to
let him know of the call on my life. He looked at me . . . shook
his head . . . and said "No, you just think that's what you want
to do." I was totally devastated. My pastor didn't believe in me
or the call on my life. It took so much strength to just go talk
to him in the first place. Suddenly, all those prophecies that
had been spoken over me, over the years, I doubted. I did push
forward, I did get my license, but it was without my pastor's
approval. I remember the day I took the test . . . I made a very
high score. I called my pastor on the way home and I asked
him . . . "Are you proud of me?" He said, "Sure I am." That was
that. I am a woman in ministry. That's a tough place to be.

IN HOLINESS, PENTECOSTAL, OR even Evangelical circles, the
need for approval is sometimes seen as a carnal or worldly desire.

Christians are to deny self, working tirelessly because of a call from God but "without honor in their own country." This kind of self-lessness is understood as virtuous and as receiving ultimate reward in heaven. In fact, it is commonly held that, if one receives honor on earth, "they've received their reward." This rhetoric distracts serious attention from the reality. Ministers—men and women—began a life-changing and challenging journey when they embrace God's call to serve as ordained clergy. It is preposterous to think such a life can be well-lived and such a calling faithfully discharged in the absence of affirmation, support, and continuing care given the nature of the pressures of ministry.

Most denominations, however, under the Holiness, Pentecostal, or Evangelical umbrella(s), including the COG, have instituted systems of ministerial credentialing that are based on affirmation and recognition of giftedness. In the COG, the process of ministerial credentialing, as interpreted in most regions, follows a particular trajectory and is overseen by the Division of Education.[1]

A person senses and expresses a "call to ministry" and shares the testimony of this call with the pastor, who then offers counsel and affirms the call, initiating the process of credentialing. This official process begins with completion of an application to apply for the initial credential, called the "Exhorter's License" (EL), and the CAMS (Calling and Ministry Studies, formerly Ministerial Affirmation Program or MAP) program, an assessment process over three months. Critical to this process is the "affirmation" of the local church pastor and the District Overseer. The CAMS exit interview determines eligibility for the EL. Approval grants the candidate permission to prepare for and complete the examination for the initiatory license. Once completing this step, the candidate completes the application for the Ordained Minister (OM) credential and the MIP (Ministerial Internship Program), a nine-month process including seminars, an internship, and CIMS (Certificate In Ministerial Studies) courses taken for college credit. The MIP process culminates in a weekend celebration and commissioning

1. "Marriage Licensure," http://www.cogdoe.org/ministries/ministerial-licensure-2/

in Cleveland, TN, the denominational headquarters, where prominent leaders affirm the candidates through the "laying on of hands." After successful completion of this process, the candidate may request and complete the OM exam. The state/regional Ministerial Development Committee and the state/regional AB are involved in this process. It could be argued that "affirmation" in this sense is a simple "stamp of approval," but given its ties to what is conceived as a spiritual rite (including laying on of hands) and confirmation of spiritual giftedness, that is a difficult case to make. Clearly the process of credentialing is meant to provide encouragement and affirmation and to express a regard of confidence in the ministerial leader. It is endorsement and commendation.

Further, the "system" affirms credentialed ministers by giving them opportunities to minister, appointments to church pastorates, elections (by their peers) and appointments (by the state and denominational leaders) to boards, public recognition for church growth, missions support, and (perhaps the highest affirmation of all) opportunities to preach at high-profile events such as prayer conferences, camp meetings, and the GA.

MYTHBUSTER:

A minister called by God does not need "man's approval."

The well-developed COG ministerial development and credentialing process is dependent upon such approval, but women ministers have limited access to it.

In light of this, it is impossible to suggest that COG ministers are not formed in a system where affirmation is needed and expected and where there is honor and reward for those meeting certain standards of success. The stories expressed by respondents to this survey reveal that while women are being credentialed and officially recognized as ministers, they do not sense that their ministry is valued or affirmed. As a result, many of these women describe a ministry environment that leads to anything but human flourishing.

Recently, Linda M. Wagener and Richard Beaton of the Max De Pree Center for Leadership have examined the concept of human flourishing from the perspective of Christian theology, concluding that humans flourish "when they routinely experience optimism, hope and gratitude and when they make a positive impact on others through their work and legacy."[2] A person derives meaning and purpose from "the awareness that the individual life is part of a larger story . . . we are connected to humanity and creation in fundamental ways."[3] What are the necessary conditions for this flourishing? They conclude, "People flourish when they have the opportunity to engage in meaningful work, have the freedom to express themselves, can engage in personal growth, have healthy reciprocal relationships and can contribute to the well-being of others."[4] When these conditions are not present, humans find themselves in a state of languishment, with "an absence of positive emotion . . . feeling empty or hollow . . . lacking confidence . . . and . . . hope."[5] Ultimately, they conclude that while languishment cannot and should not be defined as "mental illness," it may be understood as an "absence of mental health."[6]

DO COG WOMEN MINISTERS RECEIVE AFFIRMATION?

Family

Overwhelmingly, of the women answering the question of whether or not they are encouraged to pursue their ministry call by family members, 93 percent responded in the affirmative. Of the 75 percent of respondents who are married, 94 percent of them answered that they are affirmed and encouraged in ministry by their family members. Expressions of family encouragement were relatively equal

2. Wagener and Beaton, "Flourishing 101," para. 14.

3. Wagener and Beaton, "Flourishing 101," para. 15.

4. Wagener and Beaton, "Flourishing 101," para. 24.

5. Wagener and Beaton, "Flourishing 101," para. 10.

6. Wagener and Beaton, "Flourishing 101," para. 10.

across ethnic lines as well as age ranges. Several women who were daughters of COG pastors described the support given by their fathers. One pastor recalls her father's cautious support: "Because my pastor was my dad he was willing to talk to the overseer on my behalf when I told him God had spoken to me and I would pastor his church when he retired. However, he did everything in his power to talk me out of it. Not because he didn't believe I was capable or qualified, but because he knew how difficult it is to pastor as a man and thought it must surely be even harder if you are a woman."

MYTHBUSTER:

Husbands and family members oppose women ministers.

93 percent of women ministers receive the support of their family. Of those who are married, the statistic increases to 94 percent.

Pastors and Congregations

By and large, the most effective ways that pastors show affirmation of women as ministers is by giving public recognition of their call before the congregation (76 percent) and by affording them opportunities to preach (74 percent). These very public expressions of encouragement are remembered by women decades later: "When I first felt the call to preach, I went to my pastor at the time and said to him, 'What would you say if I told you I was called to preach?' He responded with 'Well, praise the Lord.' He began to use me in the pulpit without hesitation and even asked me if he could talk with other pastors, or ministers about using me."

Somewhat less encouraging are the statistics relating to the official credentialing trajectory. Approximately 70 percent report that their pastor "set them forth for ministry" before the congregation, but only 44 percent report that their pastor sponsored them for participation in the MAP (now CAMS) or the MIP. Again, the age of the respondent does not seem to be as significant a variable here as one might think, given the recent implementation of these programs. For instance, 46 percent of women from ages thirty-five to thirty-nine report that their pastor sponsored their participation, and 42 percent of those from ages sixty-five to sixty-nine report the same.

Corroborating this lack of sponsorship is the finding that only 51 percent of female ministers responding were given an explanation of the ministerial credentialing process by their pastors. Again, age does not appear to be a significant variable. Illustrating this reality is this response from a woman:

> My pastor at the time told men in the church about the COG process to become a minister; nothing was said to me. In fact, I had to pursue the information on my own and follow up with him several times about filling out the paperwork because of the constant delays.

Another reported the lack of parity in encouragement from her pastor while in the MIP, as compared to that of men in the same situation:

> When I entered the MIP program there were three other couples from my church who entered as well. The men in these couples were pursuing the COG credentialing. They were encouraged by my pastor to pursue ministry. I entered because someone from another church had made me aware of the MIP program. My pastor and his wife met each week with the three other couples. My pastor and his wife only met with my husband and me ONCE during the entire process.

Much less encouraging is the statistic that reveals that for only 32 percent of women respondents did their pastors explain educational opportunities available to them. One respondent wrote that she had "over the years, researched and studied at my own expense in the areas of ministry when I felt the need to be better equipped, to serve God's people." As one minister laments, "The only guidance I was given was when I spoke with a pastor about going to graduate school and pursuing an MDiv. He informed me most people don't do that unless they are in full-time ministry." Not only was this a discouragement from pursuing education that would likely enhance her gifting, this counsel directly implied that this female minister would never have the opportunity to serve as a full-time minister. Perhaps it indicated that he felt she should not do so. To the hearer, the discouragement was evident.

One painful memory would have to be on the very day of my graduation of the MIP ceremony. I notably recall a pastor coming up to me and telling me that I should have gone independent because this was going to lead to nothing. I also recall another story of when one of the MIP leaders told me that as a woman I will probably never get anywhere in the denomination and I should just accept this as a reality. Honestly, these words were painful at the time, but what was worse is that they are true.

In each of these areas involving "official" steps toward ministry preparation, there is some variation over lines of ethnicity. For instance, 48 percent of white respondents report sponsorship for the MAP or the MIP, while only 40 percent of Caribbean, 38 percent of African-American, and 30 percent of Hispanic respondents report sponsorship.

The experience of women is corroborated by the self-reporting of male pastors responding to the following question: "If you are a pastor, in what ways do you affirm or support the call of women to ministry?" 84 percent report giving women opportunities to preach, while only 69 percent report giving public recognition to women ministers. Where "official" responsibilities are involved, only 58 percent report that they have "set women forth for ministry"; 56 percent have explained the credentialing process to women; and only 53 percent have sponsored them for the MAP or the MIP. However, 52 percent claim that they have explained the educational opportunities available to women, in contrast to 32 percent of women who reported receiving such guidance.

When I received my Minister of Music license, my pastor at that time simply handed it to me in front of the church and said (and I quote), "Now this won't make her sing any better or play any better, it's just a step she took to better herself and open doors." It was very discouraging at the time, but I encouraged myself and pushed forward, and it has indeed opened many doors, and God has truly blessed me in my "call," and I have learned to encourage myself and allow God to do His part, and I just take care of mine.

There are, of course, other ways that their pastors or congregations may encourage young or novice ministers. One that is seemingly basic to the process is simply praying for discernment, with the person expressing their sense of call. Sadly, however, only 49 percent of women report this kind of discerning prayer took place. A higher percentage of male pastor survey respondents (60 percent) reported that this takes place in their ministry. While at first glance these findings might seem relatively positive, truthfully less than half of the women ministers received prayerful guidance from a pastor when discerning a ministry calling; these are still troubling numbers.

The news is slightly better with regard to women being given ministry opportunities within the local congregation, with 68 percent of women reporting that this occurred. This statistic is higher among Hispanic women (76 percent). The perception of male pastor respondents is that they are doing a good job of this kind of affirmation, with 80 percent reporting that they make these assignments. One Hispanic female minister recalls,

> I received both affirmation and encouragement in my call to ministry and specifically to missions. [My pastor] feeling strongly that women should be in equal ministry roles with the church, allowed me (after a vote of the congregation) to sit on the church board, which was composed of three men and three women. [My pastor] and the leadership team encouraged me to accept my role as a minister within the church and did not regard my gender as an impediment to my calling to ministry.

Interestingly, while 41 percent of women report that their pastors invited them to accompany them on ministerial visits, only 23 percent of men respondents report that they did so. Thus, only about one in five male pastor respondents made themselves available for such ministry training. This type of affirmation and mentoring experience was reported less frequently by white women (38 percent) and most frequently by Hispanic women (53 percent).

The last means of affirmation surveyed was what may be called "sponsorship." In most organizations, it is vital that those who are attempting to find their way in an organization have a "sponsor" higher up in the organization. A report in the *Harvard Business Review* (September 2010) on the 2008 Catalyst global survey of women in corporate leadership identified the need for sponsorship. Succinctly, they state, "Although women are mentored, they're not being promoted. A Catalyst study of more than 4,000 high potentials shows that more women than men have mentors— yet women are *less* likely to advance in their careers. That's because they're not actively sponsored the way the men are."[7]

Sponsors, as opposed to mentors, must be persons of influence at the senior level; they must expose their protégés to others with influence; ensure that those they sponsor are "considered for promising opportunities and challenging assignments"; "fight" or advocate for the protégé's promotion; and, importantly, they must serve to "protect" the protégé from harmful contact with those at the top or from "negative publicity."[8]

---

7. Ibarra et al., "Why Men Still Get More Promotions." See Carter, "Mentoring," http://www.catalyst.org/knowledge/mentoring-necessary-insufficient-advancement for the Catalyst study on mentoring. See Carter, "Pipeline's Broken Promise," http://www.catalyst.org/knowledge/pipelines-broken-promise, for findings of a Catalyst study revealing that women with MBAs "still lag men in advancement and compensation from their very first professional jobs and are less satisfied with their careers overall."

8. Ibarra et al., "Why Men Still Get More Promotions," 6.

Recently I attended an evening meeting of the district Church of God ministers. There were about twelve ministers present, including three that were female. The pastor of each church was asked to select the minister who would preach at the monthly district fellowship meeting when it is held at their church—they were encouraged to select non-pastor ministers (one of the four women ministers on the district is a pastor, leaving three who could have been selected). The men would look at each and select another man, never seeming to consider a female. At one point a pastor said something like "I don't know his name" and pointed at another man to select him. "Will you preach for me?" conveyed the message that a man you don't know is better than any woman. I was sitting in for our pastor, so when it was our turn I selected one of the women to preach when it was at our church. The district overseer laughed as though that was something funny and unexpected. The woman minister indicated that she would be glad to do it.

When women were asked if their pastors had affirmed them by introducing them to district or state leadership, only 41 percent could answer in the affirmative. This happens least frequently among African-Americans (37 percent). This kind of sponsorship is reported by white women at a rate of 41 percent, Caribbeans at 42 percent, and Hispanics at 51 percent. Paralleling these statistics is the self-reporting of male pastor respondents; only 44 percent claim to introduce women to leaders at the district or state levels.

DENOMINATIONAL LEADERSHIP

Given the importance of recognition by state and denominational leaders in the credentialing process, it is obvious that every minister in the COG would desire a sense of affirmation by those in authority over them and by their colleagues within a state or region. As discussed earlier, this recognition comes through official and unofficial means. Within COG culture, ministers quickly come to understand the ethos and learn the ropes. Perhaps even more important than the official recognition afforded by a certificate of ordination or even by the ordination ceremony itself is the collegiality and camaraderie, the mutual support, that is understood to exist among COG ministers. Sadly, the research conducted in this study finds that women ministers often go lacking in this kind of affirmation and feel excluded from the fellowship of ministers by virtue of their gender.

Affirmation by State/Denominational Leaders

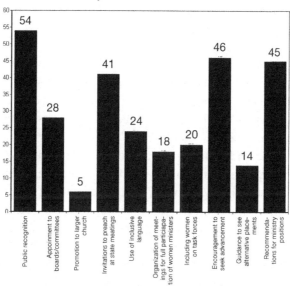

When asked, generally, if they feel affirmed by state or denominational leaders, 66 percent report that they do. Interestingly, this affirmation is seen to be less evident by male ministers surveyed, with only 58 percent seeing women as affirmed at this level. This lower estimation may be influenced by a sense that ministerial affirmation is lacking at the state or denominational levels, regardless of gender.

MYTHBUSTER:

Denominational leaders are pushing the agenda of women in ministry.

Women offer little evidence that they feel affirmed by leaders. Official denominational programs and publications cannot be shown to be supportive.

When surveying the promotional material for upcoming denominational events or support material published for ministers in the COG, one is hard-pressed to find inclusion of women ministers, even in photographs or illustrations. An analysis of the Winter 2013 edition of *Engage: A Journal for Church of God Leaders*[9] reveals that only one of twenty articles was written by a woman (Patricia Hilliard, listed as a "Coordinator of Pastoral Meals" at a Maryland congregation).[10]

Women are pictured in photographs or illustrations only three times in forty-seven pages. The first is in a line drawing for an article titled "Creating an Inviting Church Image" by Michael Knight, where they are in a group of church attendees standing outside a church and are portrayed as stylishly dressed and quite feminine, one being visibly "curvy."[11]

The second portrayal is of two female senior citizens on either side of a male senior in an article titled "Engaging Senior Adult Ministry" by Tim W. Shawyer. Given the thrust of the article, it may be assumed that these women pictured are to be seen as members of a local congregation and not as credentialed ministers.[12]

The final depiction is in an article by Anthony McDaniel titled "Family First, Church Second." Here, an African-American family is pictured engaged in prayer, with the male (pastor/husband/father) leading the prayer, holding the Bible in his hands. In this article, McDaniel refers to the pastor's family as "his family."[13]

---

9. *Engage: A Journal for Church of God Leaders* (Winter 2013), http://www.cogengage.org/. An analysis of the three previous issues revealed nearly identical findings with regard to contributions and depictions of women: Fall 2012 (1/18 articles written by a woman, all women are pictured as either wives of ministers or young students); Spring 2012 (1/22 articles written by a woman; this article was on the role of pastor's wife; only depictions of women were as wives of pastors); Winter 2012 (1/18 articles written by a woman; no depictions of women other than as church members, office staff, or wives of ministers).

10. See Hilliard, "Connecting Guests," 14–15.

11. Knight, "Creating an Inviting Church Image," 12.

12. Shawyer, "Engaging Senior Adult Ministry," 26.

13. McDaniel, "Family First," 28.

The remainder of the journal always depicts ministers, church council members, and even church members as male. No advertisements feature women in pictures. Advertisements for minister resources are for books and a DVD series with all-male authors or instructors. On page 16, he promotion for "Hydrate," a conference directed toward young missional leaders in the denomination, reveals a lineup of eleven keynote speakers and workshop leaders, all white and male.

It is difficult to conclude that there is any sort of sensitivity or intention to affirm gender, racial, or ethnic inclusivity in such presentations. At the time of this revision, a survey of the most recent issue (Winter 2018) revealed similar findings. No articles were written by women. In one advertisement for the School of Ministry on page 12, a female is pictured. But the remaining depictions of women are as congregants or in space shared with their husbands. Interestingly, the advertisement from the division of "Care Ministries" on page 23, which featured COG chaplains, depicted no women chaplains, though there are several COG-endorsed military chaplains on active duty. In an article on pages 14–16 recounting the history of Lee University, though the first principal, Nora Chambers, is mentioned, she is not pictured.[14]

Less than half of the women surveyed saw themselves as being given or directed to other ministry opportunities by state or denomination leaders. 46 percent affirm that they've received "encouragement to seek advancement in ministry rank or placement" and 45 percent report receiving recommendations for staff positions in church or ministry settings by leaders. Remarkably, only 14 percent report being "guided to seek alternative ministry

14. Fisher, "Lee University Celebrates," 14–16. Photographs of women appear in one advertisement for the Department of Evangelism's congregational training programs (p. 7) and O. Wayne and Pamela R. Brewer are pictured as Directors of Adult Discipleship (p. 17); photographs of couples appear in an advertisement for a "Marriage and Family Enrichment Cruise (p. 59). The Fall 2017 issue (http://reader.mediawiremobile.com/PathwayPress/issues/201877/viewer?page=1) fared better, with two articles out of thirteen written by women. One of those, "How a Pastor's Spouse Works with Staff" by Sandra Kay Williams, does affirm that women are called to be pastors and that not all pastors' spouses are women. (p. 52). However, depictions of women follow the same pattern.

opportunities or placements." It seems apparent that women are not being encouraged in finding either traditional (church) or alternative ministry placements.

In the COG, there is no more visible sign of affirmation or support than being asked to preach at a state or denominational meeting, such as a camp meeting service. Indeed, this is understood as a kind of public endorsement and a sign of future advancement. Only 40 percent of women responding have been given this opportunity. This sign of public affirmation is apparently more common for Hispanic women (60 percent) and least common for Caribbean (35 percent) and white women (37 percent). Ironically, 81 percent of men responded that they perceive that women are being affirmed at the state and denominational level in this way.

WHERE ARE WOMEN FINDING SUPPORT?

Friendships

The 2002/2003 survey of COG pastors conducted by the Center for Pentecostal Leadership and Care (CPLC) revealed this startling statistic: "COG pastors are three times more likely than other pastors to experience feelings of loneliness and isolation in ministry."[15]

This loneliness may be the result of geographic isolation, but is more likely to be the result of the time consumed by the stresses and demands of ministry. With 58 percent of COG female ministers surveyed reporting they work in compensated employment outside of the ministry, and 38.4 percent working in those jobs forty or more hours per week, it is a given that those demands are multiplied and the time for other relationships diminished.

Nevertheless, 94 percent of those women report having close friendships with other ministers. Who are these ministers? For one-third of them, those friendships are with other female ministers in the COG, and for another third the friendships are with male COG ministers. However, only 9 percent of male ministers reported a similar friendship with female ministers in the COG.

---

15. Bowers, *Portrait and Prospect*, 68.

Obviously, if the male minister finding is indicative of most OBs, very few are in supportive friendships with female minister peers.

Friendships with other ministers are also found outside the COG. Approximately one-fourth of women reported close friendships with female ministers outside the COG. These friendships are much more likely to be enjoyed by African-American female ministers (50 percent).

Ministry Friendships

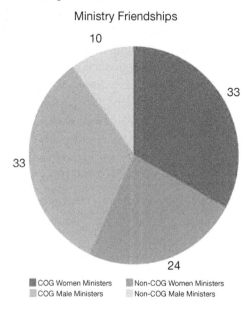

COG Women Ministers   Non-COG Women Ministers
COG Male Ministers   Non-COG Male Ministers

Support Networks

As in most denominations (and especially in those with a connectional polity), built into the COG infrastructure are programs that intentionally or informally provide relational support to ministers. These include annual meetings, educational programs, and seminars. Some are required of credentialed ministers; most are not required, but are encouraged. Obviously, the full-time minister is more able to take advantage of these opportunities. As would be expected, women ministers, many of whom are employed outside of the local church in addition to their ministerial activities, are less likely to be able to participate in such experiences.

Denominationally, the COG provides several "official" avenues for continuing engagement, fellowship, and networking for its credentialed ministers. Most regions strongly encourage attendance at the biennial state or regional "Ministers Meeting," a one-day meeting primarily for the purpose of conducting the business of the region. Additionally, many states or regions host annual retreats for ministers in the state. At the general church level, semi-regular conferences and seminars are conducted for training purposes, often utilizing speakers (published authors or consultants) from outside the denomination. Occasionally, these have been conducted in different regions of the country. In 2003, the CPLC and its "Pastoral Covenant Group" (PCG) facilitation—an initiative specifically developed for pastoral support—were launched, eventually involving around 1,000 COG pastors in the United States. This initiative was not funded after 2012. From time to time, denominational leaders have embarked upon "listening tours" in order to "listen" to the "heart" of the ministry.

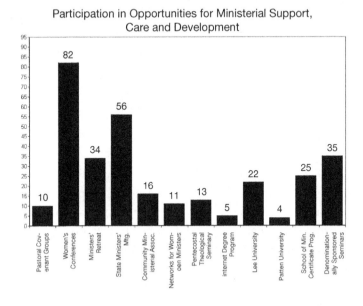

Participation in Opportunities for Ministerial Support, Care and Development

Again, as a result of the economic realities faced by women ministers, with many employed outside of the ministry, most are unable to avail themselves of these opportunities for enrichment. At the state or regional level, only 56 percent report that they have participated in the "State Ministers Meeting," as opposed to 83 percent of male ministers responding. There is no information about frequency of participation fors either female or male ministers. Given the importance of this meeting with regard to functional power in the denomination, the lack of input by credentialed women ministers is significant. Beyond this, the lack of hospitality experienced by women ministers at these meetings is detrimental to their ability to flourish. Women recall the awkwardness of attempting to find space at state ministers' meetings, often being directed to the meeting of pastors' wives being conducted by the AB's wife for the purpose of the business of the Women's Ministries department. One reported that her husband has repeatedly received invitations to meetings for pastors' wives.

Only 34 percent of women report having participated in a "ministers retreat" (the wording of the question does not specify whether or not these retreats are COG sponsored). Their male counterparts, on the other hand, attend such retreats at a rate of 57 percent. Several reported their disappointment at not being allowed to participate in the annual retreat for ministers within their state. A female evangelist, now a pastor, in a large denominational region reported that she complained about the exclusion of women from the region's major fellowship and networking event, a "retreat." The woman explained that as an evangelist, this kind of networking venue was vital for her to be able to make connections to pastors. She was informed that there was a "Women's Ministries" retreat once a year for women. This retreat, she pointed out, focuses primarily on local church auxiliary activities for women and is attended primarily by wives of male pastors and laywomen from the churches. The "Ministers' Retreat" was off-limits for any other than male ministers and was advertised as such.[16] The message is clear: women are not really considered a vital or necessary part of the clergy.

16. See the flyer for a 2017 retreat here: https://static1.squarespace.com/static/57c0c4de6a4963efc2b89f72/t/599356e1be42d66fd5658176/1502828327145/.

MYTHBUSTER:

Even though they may not be allowed to vote in the GC and serve in some official capacities, women ministers have equal opportunity for fellowship and development.

Women are actually barred from participation in retreats and find many meetings inhospitable.

Of those surveyed, only 10 percent of the female ministers had participated in a PCG (one-half of men surveyed report participation). This designated venue for peer support, while open to women ministers, wasn't a significant factor in the support of women in ministry. The factors contributing to the lack of the participation of women included the inadequate recruitment of women as group facilitators (leaders) by ABs, reluctance of women to participate in numerically male-dominated groups, and insufficient efforts of male facilitators to invite women minister participation.

COG women ministers are not finding significant sources of enrichment and support in networks of women ministers outside of the denomination (only 10.7 percent report such involvement), nor are they finding it in community ministerial associations (16 percent report involvement).

By and large, the major venue in which women participated is what is categorized as "Women's Conferences" (82 percent). These may or may not be denominationally sponsored and are likely not limited to credentialed women ministers. While they support a level of spiritual nourishment and fellowship, these conferences, ordinarily, do not address the particular needs of women ministers.

A final interesting finding with regard to ministerial development and support is that the participation of both male and female ministers in denominationally sponsored and endorsed seminars is roughly the same (35 percent). To the extent that this survey research reflects the behavior of all women and men, the responses demonstrate that these events are only attended by a minority of ministers and are, therefore, ineffective tools for ministerial development.

Mentors

Mentoring has historically been recognized as one of the most, if not *the* most, important method of preparing the less experienced member of an organization for leadership. This is accepted in the corporate world, but is also widely accepted in the church context. A Google search on "Christian spiritual mentorship" produces over eight million results. One would expect ministers to recognize the need for such a relationship for their own spiritual and professional development. For COG ministers, this is true for two-thirds of those responding to the WIM survey.

I have had a deep desire for true mentoring. Unfortunately, the men of ministry were too concerned about what it looked like on the outside for a male minister to mentor a woman minister. A woman minister doesn't even stand a chance. It is a very lonely journey, one filled with only relying on the encouragement of the Lord.

Of the women responding in the affirmative, 30 percent report having other female ministers as mentors, while male pastors have mentored 35 percent. Other responses included fathers, mothers, husbands, and grandfathers who were ministers and mentors. 65 percent of men who responded to the survey claim to have mentored women in the ministry, while only 5 percent of them report having been mentored by a woman minister.

Descriptions of Mentors of Women Ministers

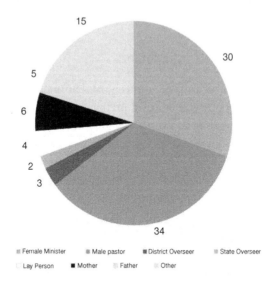

Female Minister   Male pastor   District Overseer   State Overseer
Lay Person   Mother   Father   Other

Clearly, the majority of women recognize the need for such mentorship and are finding mentors in some way. While the COG credentialing process requires being formally acknowledged and recommended by both the local and district pastor, and the MIP supervision is provided by a pastor, only one-third of these women reporting that they are in a mentoring relationship are being mentored by male pastors who make up approximately 97 percent of COG pastors in the United States. Mentoring is understood to be a significant and real need for these women. Still, one-third of respondents have not received that kind of spiritual formation. As one woman reported, "I feel like I've fallen through the cracks." Another wrote, "My pastor doesn't help me very much. He is busy building a mega-church."

Role Models

One of the important ways that women, especially women ministers, own their call and vocation is by imagining themselves in that role. Without a "mirror image" of what she may become—a woman in ministerial leadership—it is difficult for a woman to visualize herself in that position, and the pursuit of her vocation becomes more difficult if not impossible.

MYTHBUSTER:

Women look to high-profile evangelists and televangelists as role models.

Local and lesser known women evangelists and pastors are most often named as role models by COG women ministers.

When asked what woman minister has been a role model for them, 472 women responded with a wide variety of answers. Women listed the names of many women pastors, evangelists, and teachers, most within the COG but also from outside. Most of these women cited as role models of ministry were only cited once. For the most part, even the more well-known COG female evangelists or pastors (Jackie McCullough, Jackie Smith, Kathy Hamon, Jocelyn Barnett) had fewer than five mentions; this was also true of prominent women in the larger Pentecostal arena (Kathryn Kuhlman, Anne Giminez). There were two exceptions. The most often-mentioned role model was television preacher-teacher Joyce Meyer, though she was only cited thirty-seven times. Mentioned twelve times was COG minister Annette Watson, who has preached in many women's conferences throughout the COG. The other prominent mention was of mothers or grandmothers as role models (twenty-six citations).

What can be concluded from these disparate findings? It appears that local and lesser known women ministers have had the most impact as role models for women ministers in the COG. This may be seen as a positive and healthy finding with regard to the significance of local role models for the formation of women ministers. What is noteworthy is that it may be said that there are no "prominent" or high-profile women in the COG who surface as major role models. For those looking outside of their locality,

Joyce Meyer and her message of victorious Christian living provides a vision of who they can be.

CONCLUSIONS: WHAT IS THE SUPPORT NET?

Given these findings, it must be concluded that the primary support net for women ministers in the COG consists of their affirming family and their friendships with other women, inside and outside of the COG. It can be fairly concluded that they find little real encouragement for their ministry from the leadership of the denomination, or even from fellow male ministers. Further, women are not finding peer support or structured mentoring outside of the denomination in any intentional way. The reasons for this were not clearly stated, but it is likely that the same factors are at work: lack of hospitality and financial freedom to access support.

A RESPONSE: SABRINA EVANS, BA, MA, MACMHC (CLINICAL MENTAL HEALTH COUNSELING)

COG Career Missionary, Prague, Czech Republic

As I read this chapter through the lens of being a counselor and a single female missionary, it causes me to reflect on my first year in ministry. Fortunately, my first placement was to serve on a church-planting team under egalitarian leadership. Following a leadership meeting, I held a conversation with my team leader and shared ideas I thought were vital to our church plant. The response to my ideas was extremely positive, yet I was asked why I did not present them to the rest of the team. As I expressed a lack of confidence and uncertainty about my role, I found myself facing a soft rebuke. I was encouraged that my gifts were not my own, but they were given for the building up of God's kingdom. I learned the difference between practicing true humility and suppressing my gifts.

In the months to come, I found my voice and it was met with affirmation and guidance. At times, I was asked to lead service or head an event. The feedback I received afterwards was as equally vital to my formation as the opportunity itself. My mentors were mirrors. They reflected back to me untapped strengths, as well as areas where I needed to improve. I could not have seen myself clearly or discerned my calling apart from these role models, male and female. While it is unhealthy to attain our entire identity in the eyes of others, it is equally unhealthy to expect someone to develop and flourish apart from the role of a supportive spiritual community. As beings formed in the image of a communal God, it is simply how we are designed.

It saddens me on multiple levels to know that my example is exceptional. As a counselor, I am always concerned with the flourishing of the individual; as a missionary, I am always concerned with the reaping of the harvest. Pointing back to the lesson I learned in my first year of ministry, our gifts are given for the work of God's kingdom. Through living and serving in the atheistic capital of Europe, I am daily faced with the reality that the harvest is plentiful, but the laborers few. From the perspective of the harvest field, we cannot afford to have half of our laborers languishing. This chapter is an urgent call to provide the support necessary for all of our ministers to flourish equally and to be sent forth in expectation of their full potential.

A RESPONSE: REV. MIA PITTMAN-HEAD, MA (CANDIDATE)

Senior Pastor, Omega Harvest Church, Red Bank, TN

As I have been so impressed with the writing style, passion, and comprehensive content of previous monographs by Dr. James Bowers and Dr. Kimberly Alexander, it was with great anticipation I received their latest work. Just a small portion was offered for my consumption, but it was very filling. However, no fillers were used in the recipe of this script, and I quickly realized a sharp knife and fork would be needed to consume the meat of this offering.

Chapter 4 opens with the following question: are women flourishing as ministers? It then quickly moves to the recalled memory of one woman who anticipated the calling of God upon her life, but when she shares this anticipation with her pastor, his affirmation is withheld but his distain is offered freely. Although this was a memory, the conclusion of this chapter brings the material full circle. It reveals that no real intentionality exists, even to this day, in the vital areas of peer support and structured mentoring needed for the women minister to flourish. As I read, I kept looking for a sign saying "Warning: Content Not Suitable for The Immature!"

Moving through the deep waters of this chapter, I felt my excitement met from time to time with the jagged rocks of sadness and pain, brought on by the sheer magnitude of the staggering statistical information provided. My proverbial boat might have capsized if not for the comfort of the Holy Spirit and the knowledge that this writing would help to right the boat and bring further movement.

Many times this script reminded me of the genealogy chapters contained within Holy Scripture. Statistic after statistic was offered, and I began to feel the all too familiar urge to skip over it in an attempt to just get to the good part. But as with Holy Scripture, these statistics were not meant to be skipped over because they are vital to the telling of the story. To skip over them would, once again, rob and withhold from them the affirmation due them. So I read it all. And I read it again. I continued to receive each page of this material and as I did, a profound and deep awareness washed over me. These statistics represented human life; each situation a living, breathing soul. Captured within the focus of my reading was the answer to the initial question. It was no longer so far off in the distance, but as it moved closer and closer to me, the sound of its voice was almost deafening. In order for something to flourish, it must be fed. And if this is true (and it is), then the opposite is also true. The voice spoke again with the word "languishment" on its tongue; languishment felt within the heart of the starving women minister.

Peering into the waters of this chapter, an understanding is gained. Recognition does not equal affirmation, just as desegregation does not equal equality. Recognition offers credit for tasks completed, but affirmation offers confidence. Affirmation offers credibility. Affirmation offers opportunity. Affirmation is essential; it is a necessary nutrient needed to feed and bring health to any minister, male or female. However, if affirmation is withheld, as the evidence shows in the case of the women minister, one should not be surprised or embarrassed by the bloated belly of the malnutrition its absence has most certainly caused. So what is one to do when presented with the evidence of ministerial malnutrition? My answer is this: give the women something to eat! And in the offering, as with this chapter, health will be restored, strength will be renewed, and much will accomplished for the cause of Christ!

Chapter 5

What Women Can Expect in Compensation and Advancement

*My observation after thirty-two years in ministry has been
that no matter how qualified and prepared, educated and
equipped a woman is, the male will be used first. He will be
recognized and she will be expected to "stay in her place."*

DESPITE THE EMPIRICALLY VERIFIED and well-described value—if
not superior functioning—of women in leadership, women continue to trail their male counterparts doing similar work in advancement opportunities and compensation.[1] Only 14 percent of
senior executive leadership positions in Fortune 500 companies
are held by women, and in the United States, the "gender pay gap"
means that women make 77.5 percent of what men engaged in
similar work earn.[2] Certain WIM survey questions answered by
respondents provide data useful for constructing a portrait of
the compensation and advancement opportunities for women in

1. See Swartz, "What Women Know." See also Zenger and Folkman, "Are
Women Better Leaders?"
2. *Women in the Labor Force: A Databook.*

Pentecostal ministry. How do women ministers compare to men in compensation and benefits for their ministry service? How likely are women to be bi-vocational ministers? In what kinds of ministry placements do women serve? Are women ministers provided advancement opportunities afforded to men? What do women really want in these areas?

HOW WELL ARE WOMEN MINISTERS COMPENSATED?

Several questions in the WIM survey provide perspective on the compensation of Pentecostal women ministers in the COG. Of those responding to the question asking what amount represented their personal annual ministerial compensation, the largest group—65 percent—indicated they earn $5,000 or less annually. Shockingly, nearly 80 percent of the female ministers surveyed claimed to earn less than $20,000 annually from ministerial service. Fewer than five percent (4 percent) reported earning $50,000 each year. By contrast, of the male OBs responding to the same question, only 12 percent made $5,000 or less, and fewer than 20 percent earned less than $20,000 annually. So, more than 80 percent of female ministers earn less than $20,000 dollars, while 80 percent of men ministers surveyed earn more than $20,000 dollars.

Another way to view women's compensation is to note that the approximate median annual income for male OBs is between $40,000–44,999, while the approximate annual median income for female ministers is much less than $5,000.[3] Nearly two-thirds of

---

3. Given the separation of salary from housing and other benefits in the COG salary schedule for pastors, it can be safely assumed these compensation figures do not include such provisions as a housing allowance/parsonage, Social Security, hospitalization insurance, pension contributions and other special gifts. See the COG salary schedule for pastors in Appendix 3. Full-time pastors are expected to receive housing (often including utilities), one-half of Social Security, hospitalization insurance premiums for the pastor and family, and a minimum 5 percent of salary pension contribution. While all male pastors falling into the median annual income do not receive all these benefits, responses to other questions indicate that far more men than women do receive

female ministers—62 percent—report receiving no compensation for the ministry work they do, as compared with 15 percent of male OB survey respondents. Additionally, nearly three-fourths (or 74 percent) of women report working part-time in ministry, compared to 40 percent of male OBs surveyed.

MYTHBUSTER:

Compensation guidelines apply equally to men and women ministers.

Most women ministers actually receive no compensation or work part-time in ministry, and receive less than $5,000 annually and no benefits.

Other disparities and inequities are found when women ministers and male OBs are compared with regard to fringe benefits and important compensatory provisions like housing allowances. The housing allowance provision—which results in substantial tax savings for ministers—is virtually non-existent for female ministers, with 84 percent of those surveyed reporting that they do not receive this allowance, compared to 41 percent of the male OBs who responded to the survey. Therefore, female ministers are twice as likely as their male survey counterparts *not* to receive a housing allowance. Additionally, a comparable 88 percent of women reported non-participation in the denominational ministerial pension plan compared to 47 percent of men surveyed. Participation rates in non-denominational pension plans were comparable between women (39 percent) and men (42 percent). Women not participating in the denominational ministerial pension plan were much more likely (91 percent) than non-participating men surveyed (54 percent) not to have the housing allowance provided.

---

them. The median income figures here are estimates based on the number of women and men who are in each salary range. An exact median could not be figured because ranges of income were reported, not exact salary amounts.

Personal Annual Ministerial Compensation

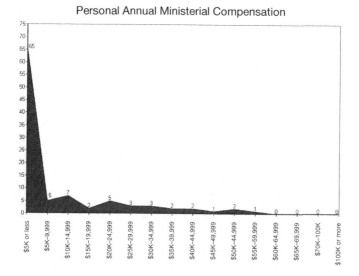

What emerges from these survey findings is a picture of Pentecostal women ministers as the economic underclass in relation to their male counterpart OBs. A woman minister is six times more likely to make $5,000 or less annually than a male minister surveyed and four times more likely to never make more than $20,000 a year. In fact, a woman is four times more likely to receive no compensation. The same woman is also about twice as likely to be part-time in ministry, receive no housing allowance, and have no denominationally sponsored or church-funded pension for her service. As inequitable as compensation for women generally is in American society, from a compensation perspective, survey results indicate that credentialed Pentecostal women ministers in the COG are much more economically disadvantaged in comparison to their male minister counterparts.

HOW LIKELY ARE WOMEN TO BE BI-VOCATIONAL MINISTERS?

Given the previous discussion of compensation for Pentecostal women ministers in the COG, it is not surprising to find survey responses confirming the virtual certainty that women will be bi-vocational ministers. Actually, 58 percent of female ministers reported that they "work in compensated employment outside the ministry," and 62 percent of all female ministers reported they are not "compensated for ministry." An even larger proportion—72 percent—of those compensated for non-ministerial work report receiving no compensation for ministry. In comparison, 32 percent of male OB respondents reported "work in compensated employment outside the ministry," and just 15 percent of all male OBs reported that they are not "compensated for ministry" work. Further, among male OBs who are compensated outside ministry, only 31 percent claim to receive no remuneration for their ministry. Assuming a base COG pastor's compensation package for a church of twenty-five to one hundred members with salary, housing, and other fringe benefits of approximately $67,000–75,000 annually, less than 4 percent of the Pentecostal COG women minister respondents indicated they receive such income compared to 16 percent of male COG OB respondents.[4] Of course, 52 percent of male OB respondents receive this level of compensation or more compared to only 8 percent of women.

While the overall picture of ministerial compensation for COG ministers of either gender isn't exceptionally positive, the great disparity between men and women in the broader income picture creates a greater probability that women will be bi-vocational ministers. Consider again, as further elaboration on earlier compensation data, that 77 percent of women compared to 23 percent of men reported ministerial incomes of $5,000 or less, 89 percent of women reported ministerial incomes of less than $20,000 compared to 37 percent of men, and 95 percent of women

4. According to the COG salary/compensation schedule for pastors, a pastor with one to twenty-five members is to receive $40,612 (salary), while a pastor with at least one hundred members is due $47,788 (salary). Housing is also to be provided, and is conservatively estimated to be equivalent to $12,000 annually. Hospitalization insurance will typically be provided and represent minimally $9,600 each year. Pension is typically 5 percent of salary, and one-half Social Security is figured at 7.5 percent, equaling another $5,076.50 to $5,973 for twenty-five members and one hundred members per pastor, respectively. See Appendix 3.

report earning less than $30,000 annually compared to 60 percent of men respondents. The survey data indicates that compensation of Pentecostal women ministers in the COG is dramatically less than their male counterparts even though other factors such as church size (although males pastor more larger churches), tenure and education are relatively equivalent. This data suggests that Pentecostal women ministers in the COG are much more likely— almost two to one—to be bi-vocational ministers than their male OB colleagues if we understand bi-vocational ministry to refer to the necessity to pursue compensation outside one's primary ministerial vocation in order to meet livelihood needs.

Comensated for Ministry?

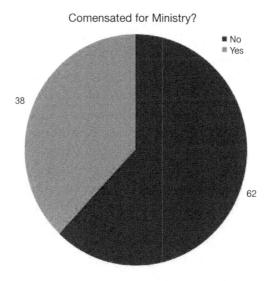

■ No
▩ Yes

38

62

HOW AND WHERE ARE WOMEN PLACED IN MINISTRY?

Naturally, there is a relationship between issues of compensation and the kinds of ministry placements women and men find in pursuit of their vocation. Of the various ministry roles in which women serve, only 11 percent of survey respondents reported "Lead Pastor" as their "current ministry title." The primary ministry post for male OBs was "Lead Pastor" with 92 percent of respondents claiming that title. The largest percentage of female ministers—17 percent—serve with the title of "Evangelist." This no doubt reflects the historical acceptance of "women preachers" and preaching as a safe zone for women in ministry that avoids the conflicts frequently voiced concerning women serving in administrative leadership. As has been noted by others, strangely, the women serving as "Associate Pastor" (11 percent), "Co-Pastor" (7 percent), "Assistant Pastor" (5 percent) and "Chaplains" (4 percent) are not seen as violating administrative leadership boundaries. While women report serving in many ministry capacities, male OB respondents are overwhelmingly "Lead Pastors" with only 3 percent serving as "Co-Pastor" and a lesser number in other staff positions (Minister of Music, Christian Education, Educational Administrator).

Of the women ministers serving as "Lead Pastors," most arrived at their ministry post without the usual pastoral appointment process involving a COG AB. Only 42 percent of Pentecostal women pastors in the COG indicated they came to their congregation by virtue of appointment by the state AB. Most reported becoming a senior pastor by planting their own church (48 percent). Others referred to moving from a staff position to pastor the same congregation (7 percent), succeeding a deceased spouse (1 percent), or assuming the reins of the church when their father retired or resigned (3 percent). By comparison, 82 percent of male OB respondents reported being appointed by the State AB and only 16 percent planted a church. Another small number became pastors by moving from a staff position into the role (1 percent) or taking over when their fathers retired or resigned (1 percent).[5]

---

5. Though the polity is different than that of the COG, Alminana and Olena describe a similar situation in the Assemblies of God in the US: "Today, in the Assemblies of God, a woman has an extremely rare prospect of being placed into a senior pastorate by the denomination or by a thriving church whether large or small." (Alminana and Olena, p. 72.)

MYTHBUSTER:

Evangelism and church planting efforts are being led by male ministers.

Women are actually more likely to serve as evangelists and church planters.

As the accounts of many women ministers indicate, a major obstacle to women being considered for appointment to more pastoral positions is the implicit and, often, explicitly expressed sexism regarding the role/s of women. One female minister relayed the following story:

> I was appointed by a previous overseer to a board that consisted of me and several other pastors. I was immediately "given" the job of "secretary." I certainly don't mind taking notes, but there is an underlying attitude there that suggests that if a woman is present then she is the one qualified to takes notes and make coffee. What did they do before I arrived? Again, I did not mind at all. I will serve however I can to advance the kingdom and do so joyfully, but my point is to reveal attitudes that will hinder the advancement of the kingdom through the COG.

Many other stories relayed by women ministers tell of being passed over for ministry opportunities, not being considered for better church pastorates, being placed on state meeting schedules to speak at times when few persons would be present and not being considered in meeting planning.

WHAT OPPORTUNITIES FOR ADVANCEMENT IN MINISTRY DO WOMEN HAVE?

The WIM survey also asked Pentecostal women minister respondents questions related to their opportunities for professional advancement. When asked if they were "encouraged to seek advancement in ministry rank or placement" by state and denominational leaders, 45 percent of women responded affirmatively and about the same number (45 percent) report being "recommended for ministry staff positions in churches or other ministry settings." Having nearly half of female ministers encouraged to pursue advancement and recommended for ministry positions initially appears to be a somewhat positive finding.

Promotion to a Larger Congregation

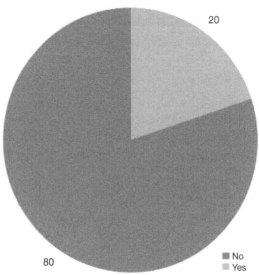

An examination of other advancement indicators, however, reveals a largely discordant reality for women. For example, just 18 percent of women say state or denominational meetings are organized for the "full participation of women ministers." This would lead to less visibility—and only 54 percent of women report any kind of public recognition in such meetings—and, consequently, less likelihood of advancement. In fact, very few women—only 20 percent—report serving as "members of special task forces," or "ever being promoted from a smaller to a larger church," and only slightly more (28 percent) have been appointed to "state or denominational boards or committees." Perhaps most telling are responses indicating that only 14 percent of women are actually "guided to find alternative ministry opportunities or placements," and just 6 percent report being specifically affirmed by leadership by being promoted to "larger or more viable congregations."[6]

MYTHBUSTER:

Women are encouraged to seek advancement in ministry rank and placement.

Women are offered little or no guidance for viable paths for advancement, and few (7 percent) have ever been promoted to a larger congregation.

As discouraging as this advancement picture is for Pentecostal women ministers, correlation of certain data leads to a more disturbing scenario. For women actually encouraged to "seek advancement in ministry rank or placement," there is little difference in markers of advancement opportunity. Just slightly more—23 percent—say that state and denominational meetings are organized for their full participation, and no more report experiencing public recognition in such meetings. Again, slightly more report serving "as members of special task forces" (27 percent) and being appointed to "state or denominational boards and committees" (26 percent). But in the important area of receiving guidance to find alternative ministry opportunities or placements, there is virtually no difference (18 percent), nor in being promoted to "larger and more viable congregations" (7 percent) by state/denominational leaders. All of this indicates that, even for women ministers who report that they were encouraged by state and denominational leaders to seek advancement in ministry rank or placement, the likelihood of advancement was no better than for those who reported no such encouragement.

For the most part, I do not attend Ministers' Meetings, etc., because they are aimed at the men [sic] ministers and their wives. My husband is not my wife. In his own words, he considers the COG "a white, good ol' boys club" and has pretty much had it with the denomination.

When factors such as tenure of ministerial service and educational preparation are considered, there are positive and negative correlations for advancement. Perhaps not surprisingly, women who hold an earned college degree are more likely to be "guided to find alternative ministry opportunities or placements." In fact, all the women receiving such guidance reported holding at least an associate's degree but, again, only 14 percent of all women ministers surveyed had such experiences. Given the small percentage of women serving as "Lead Pastors" (12 percent), many have been guided to lesser-paying church staff positions (Associate Pastor, Assistant Pastor, Children's Pastor, etc.), and approximately one-fifth are serving outside the local church. Of the 6 percent of women ministers promoted to "larger or more viable congregations," 68.18 percent held at least a college degree, with most having bachelor's degrees (32 percent). College-educated women ministers were also encouraged to seek advancement (60 percent) and were recommended for ministry positions in churches and other settings (61 percent). While the prospects for advancement for women, therefore, is bleak, those most likely to find opportunities—if outside church ministry—are those who are better educated. The data also revealed that, of the few women ministers promoted from a smaller to a larger congregational pastorate, most had been in ministry for approximately a decade.

MYTHBUSTER:

Men are better educated for ministry than women.

Women are actually as well-educated as men, with approximately two-thirds of both genders surveyed having at least a college degree.

CONCLUSION: WHAT DO WOMEN REALLY WANT?

From the data discussed in this chapter on the experience of Pentecostal COG women ministers, certain conclusions are suggested for how women need or want to be better affirmed in the areas of compensation, placement, and advancement. Clearly, women want more equitable and adequate compensation for ministry compared to their male colleagues. While bi-vocational ministry is a more likely reality for all COG ministers, women experience levels of remuneration that impair their ability to provide for their needs, consider full-time ministry, or participate in professional development and fringe benefits accorded to male ministers. Ministry as one's primary or exclusive source of livelihood for women is almost certain to mean living a life of poverty.

Placement is also problematic for women ministers. Most know they are unlikely to be appointed to a pastorate—unless it is a failing church no man wants—and must plant a church if they are to pastor. If this missional area is the best route for women to become pastors, women need and want more support and development for the challenge. Given the verbal emphasis on church planting among Pentecostals and other Christian groups, a focused initiative to empower women as church planters would be welcomed by women and strategically wise for mission. Scholarship support for women to pursue ministerial training is also important, as education provides women called to ministry more options for meaningful service. Concerted efforts also are needed to sensitize administrative bishops and other denominational leaders to support women's consideration for pastorates and other ministry posts.

Women also need real opportunities to advance in ministry. Reorganizing state and denominational meetings to be gender-inclusive—not assuming all ministers are male—and highlighting the contributions of women in clergy leadership as well as giving them more visibility on boards, committees, and in state/denominational functions is desperately needed. Often noted "good intentions" and verbal encouragement for advancement in ministry only further damage women's faith in the church and their self-esteem in the absence of tangible sponsorship for their real progress and presence in better ministry settings. Women do not want more "encouragement talk"; rather, they want to see tangible action to give them equal opportunity for advancement and a living wage.

A RESPONSE: REV. PEGGY MADDEN HARMANN, BA, MADCF

Chaplain, Cookeville Regional Medical Center, Cookeville, TN

A women's conference in the eighties provided my first encounter with women ministers and their role in the COG. There were amazing testimonies of ministry and churches established with their leadership. Their accounts of resistance within the church were disturbing, as ministry was restricted for very capable, anointed members of the body of Christ. This led me to begin studying beyond my "proof texts" about the role of women in the church.

Before retiring, I worked for thirty years in a Fortune 500 company in various roles, including Global Vice-President. An important part of our leadership work was to assure equity of compensation, including salary and benefits. Compensation generally reflects the value that the one paying places on the work of the individual. When an individual is paid more or less than others, a message is given, intentional or not, about their relative value.

As I reviewed the summary provided in this chapter, I concluded that the data reflects that women are generally poorly compensated and encounter significant hindrances in moving toward leadership roles. The study highlights factors which affect compensation indirectly, beyond the ordination issue, such as exclusion of women from ministers' meetings, perceived support from leaders, and lack of visibility for women as valued ministers in key events and groups.

As a seminary graduate and credentialed minister, my concern is for fellow women ministers and those who would be blessed by their ministry. During a recent ministers' meeting, I expressed surprise that women were excluded from a state ministers' meeting, and I was told by the leader present to "call BR549 and talk to someone who cares." Such comments and the data herein reflect a need for significant, further valuing of all ministers.

A RESPONSE: REV. DIANE MANN, DMIN

*Lead Pastor, 4th Avenue International Worship Center,
Ft. Lauderdale, FL*

"What Women Can Expect in Compensation and Advancement" is indeed a chapter that issues a clarion call for a definitive change in the perception and placement of women in ministry by the hierarchal system of the COG. The statistics given, based on research that reflects the realities of the life experiences of the women in ministry surveyed and their male counterparts, were brutally honest and revealing of the inequities that, according to the stark evidence, prevail for women ministers. The implications, if not corrected by being strategic and intentional, are staggering for the future of affirmation, placement, and the advancement of the next generation of women in ministry.

It is true that the perceived almost always becomes the reality. Personally, I sit somewhere in the middle of the reality of the statistics given. Early on in my ministry, I was privileged to meet an elderly evangelist who shared insight from her life as a woman in ministry. Her stories, though she has now reached her eternal reward and crown of glory, are forever etched in my mind, and are most certainly mirrored in the stark and brutally honest statistics found in this volume. Her revival meetings bore great spiritual success, but her struggles precipitated by the lack of equitable financial compensation cannot be ignored. Upon hearing her stories, I was compelled to reevaluate, and at the same time reaffirm my choices to be devoted to a life of ministry—not only as a calling, but also as a profession.

After more than thirty years of ministry, sixteen of those as a lead pastor, I have concluded that it is necessary for change to come. I am grateful for every opportunity that has been given me. From the AB who first encouraged me to pursue my license as a "Minister of Music" to the AB who assigned me as the lead pastor of the 4th Avenue International Worship Center (COG), I am thankful for the role they played in my advancement. I am most appreciative of a father, also a pastor, who encouraged me to "be obedient to the heavenly vision" and not focus on my gender, as opposed to my calling.

That said, I still remember how it felt as an evangelist on Evangelism Day as the "evangelists" in our green coats were introduced at a camp-meeting service, to hear the moderator ask the "brothers to please stand." I looked at the only other woman evangelist on the platform, smiled, and quietly said, "I am not now nor ever will be a brother." In times past, it was a common occurrence for me to receive a letter from the state office inviting the pastors and their wives to a state function or meeting. I'll never forget that, on one of those occasions, I picked up the phone and called a friend who worked there and shared the fact that "I do not now nor will I ever have a wife." She sheepishly explained to me that it was a form letter. As far as compensation is concerned I, like many of my female colleagues, realize that there are definite disparities between our situation and that of our male counterparts. My prayer is that this report will be read by those who can make change and that we, with grace, will continue to follow our calling, while at the same time be voices—not only for those in ministry now, but for the generations to come.

Chapter 6

A Portrait of a Pentecostal Woman Minister

I personally have struggled hard in my ministry, with only one dear pastor friend encouraging me in my ministry, not to mention my husband, the main encouraging figure in my life. I don't know why my own pastor does not. Very disappointed with several things over the years that have happened, all the while trying my best to keep the right attitude and not go somewhere else. Thinking all the while I'm being tested like Joseph. But [it] would really be nice if I did have the support and encouragement from my own pastor. My husband even admitted it would have been easier if I had been a man.

AFTER HEARING THE VOICES of 726 credentialed Pentecostal women ministers in the COG from across the United States reflecting a cross-section of age, ethnicity, and educational preparation, a profile or picture of the prototypical women minister has emerged. The portrait is simultaneously surprising, disturbing, and endearing.

WHO IS SHE?

Like her male counterparts in the COG, the Pentecostal women minister is most likely white and politically conservative. She is married and usually middle-aged, somewhere between the ages of forty and sixty-four.[1] She has attended college and is likely to have completed a Bachelor's or Master's degree. Her views on the role of women and men in the home do not vary appreciably from male ministers given her predominant affirmation that "men are the scripturally designated priests of the home."

The woman minister readily self-identifies theologically and experientially as a Pentecostal. She fulfills her ministerial call either as an evangelist, pastor, or associate pastor.

If a pastor, she is about three times more likely to have planted her church than the male Pentecostal pastor in the same town or region.

Like the majority of congregations across the denominational spectrum in the United States, her congregation is under seventy-five members. She has been pastor of her congregation for over ten years. She has most likely never been promoted in ministry from a smaller to a larger congregation and, if past history is any indication, in all probability cannot expect that kind of advancement.

Compared to most of her male counterparts, she is twice as likely to work twenty to fifty hours in a job outside of the church or ministry in which she is employed. In addition, she works up to twenty hours a week in ministry, for which she is usually compensated $5,000 or less annually. She is as likely as her male counterpart to be college-educated but, as is generally true for women in American society, earns much less than men (and far below the

1. The percentage of women ministers falling into the age range of forty to sixty-four (69.2 percent) roughly compares to male ministers (79 percent). Men and women minister respondents under forty represented a relatively small percentage (12.2 percent and 18.5 percent respectively). These demographics cannot be directly compared to the 2002–2003 survey of COG senior pastors because that survey included women and men, was not limited to OBs (among men) and did not include other ministers who were not senior pastors.

median salary for her educational level).[2] It is more likely that she receives no compensation at all. She does not receive a housing allowance, and is most often not a participant in any sort of pension program, church-sponsored or otherwise.

When she expressed her call to ministry, she received some encouragement from her pastor. There was public acknowledgement as she was given opportunities to preach, and was recognized and set forth for ministry before the congregation. She was assigned some ministry tasks in the congregation. It is less probable that she received spiritual direction in helping her to discern her call, or that she benefited from supportive prayer. Even less likely was the offering of guidance toward further ministerial development, such as the credentialing process or educational opportunities.

She was not "sponsored" by her pastor or introduced to state or denominational leaders. While there may have been some sort of public recognition of her ministry at a state or denominational meeting, it is highly unlikely that she was given the opportunity to preach or address those meetings. She has rarely, if ever, been appointed to any board or committee. Her denominational leaders have not recommended her for ministerial positions in the state or region. In fact, she has often felt out of place, lost, or even excluded in those meetings as a result of the gender exclusive language used to refer to ministers. Sadly, this pastor or evangelist has not been invited to be a participant in retreats for ministers, denying her the opportunity for both networking and fellowship. In all likelihood, she has attended retreats and conferences for women sponsored by the denomination's "Women's Ministries" department, but has found that to be a place more geared toward the non-credentialed women in her church. She has not been invited to participate in a denominationally sponsored PCG where she could find support, friendship, and further ministerial development.

2. According to the National Center for Education Statistics website, for the year 2010 the median annual income for a female with an associate's to bachelor's degree was $37,770–$47,440, respectively. Over two-thirds of the women surveyed—as was true for the men surveyed—held at least an associate's degree, with most having more advanced degrees (National Center for Education Statistics, "Median Annual Earnings").

Fortunately, she has found affirmation in her family and in friendships with other ministers, both male and female, both inside and outside the COG. She may have a mentor who is a male or female minister. She has found role models for ministry in the women pastors and evangelists she has known at the local level and from her mother or grandmother. However, she cannot point to prominent women ministers in the COG who have inspired her to become who she is called to be as a minister. She may look to women outside the denomination for that modeling; the most likely place that woman will be found is in a television ministry.

WHAT DOES SHE WANT?

Simply put, she wants to fulfill her call and vocation. She believes that the Scripture she values supports her serving as an OB in the church. Further, she believes that she is qualified and is capable for the role. She thinks she should be able to participate in the business of the church at every level: the GC, state leadership, and denominational leadership. In spite of COG polity restrictions and teaching, she sees no scriptural warrant for her non-participation in all levels of the business administration of the church. At the local level, she believes she should and could function at the senior pastor level. She sees no scriptural reason why women should not serve in any leadership position traditionally held by men in the COG. The only real obstacles to her being able to do so are attitudes and beliefs held by denominational leaders, congregations, and male ministers in the COG. By and large, she believes that the scriptural view is that women and men have full and equal authority in the church.

WHAT DOES SHE NEED?

While it is helpful to describe this prototypical Pentecostal woman minister in an attempt to understand her status and what her expectations might be, it is equally important to consider what is needed for this minister and her 3,000-plus sisters in the COG, as well as the thousands of sisters ministering within the larger Pentecostal community in the United States and beyond. After careful analysis of the data and listening to the stories of these women, seven primary recommendations can be made.

First, she needs to be heard and included in the conversations about gender and ministry. While this survey has given women an opportunity to voice their beliefs and to describe their plight, and while some scholars have written and published articles and books calling for full participation of women, the polity of the COG and that of other Pentecostal fellowships most often prohibits women from being a part of the very conversation that determines their present and future participation in the church. It must be noted and acknowledged by male ministers and denominational leaders that there is no defensible reason why women ministers have not been engaged in conversation about their lives, needs, and ministries, even outside the official meetings of the church from which they are excluded. That this has not been done is an indication of the lack of concern for women ministers in the COG.[3] Given the low compensation and resulting economic status, women ministers lack sufficient resources and power to impact the system that determines their vocational opportunity. In the COG, they are placed in a situation of dependency upon male OBs and are literally silenced by the restrictions at issue. Without a seat in the conversation, women ministers are not heard and find themselves in the humiliating position of the beggar asking for crumbs from the men-only table of decision-making.

Second, there is a need for recognition that her pursuit of full empowerment in ministry leadership is not motivated by any desire to undermine traditional family values or necessarily associated with any liberal political leanings. On the contrary, as indicated

---

3. Interestingly, after this study was completed and became public knowledge, the US Missions Division of the COG announced a denominational conference focusing on women ministers to be held in August of 2013 (see http://www.faithnews.cc/?p=14081).

by a comparison with the male OB survey respondents, women's views on family and their political orientation are very similar to that of male ministers. The assumptions that have been made in heated debates with regard to these women's so-called "liberal feminist agenda" leading to the demise of the family are faulty and only serve to further polarize the discussion; additionally, this vitriolic language is intended to paint a picture of women as dangerous to the cherished conservative identity of many of the denominational adherents. In fact, it rather seems that male OBs are most likely surrendering the empowerment implications of Pentecostal experience for all persons—regardless of gender—to a "family values" agenda of an external culture war that promotes male dominance as the lynchpin to marital, familial, and church health.

Third, there must be affirmation of her emotional confidence, educational preparedness, and ministerial experience necessary for opportunities for service at all levels of leadership. With both education and experience equivalent to her male counterparts, the female minister is confident that she is capable of leading both congregations and state and denominational ministries. Again, it is simply misguided to see her as being emotionally insecure in her abilities or unable to handle administrative leadership. Misguided as it is, male OBs who affirm the ability of women to lead (after all, they support such leadership in the civic and governmental arena), and are at least ambivalent on the question of whether Scripture restricts their leadership, do tend to think of women as emotionally less stable for senior leadership roles open to OB status. This stereotype of women has a long history and has led some recent observers to call for women to exhibit more aggressively male traits in order to succeed in corporate contexts, but the assumption that so-called "feminine" psychology is counterproductive to effective leadership remains open to debate.[4]

Fourth, there is a real need for a conversation about how she reads Scripture differently on the question of gender and ministry leadership than does her male counterpart. The female minister sees no scriptural prohibition for her serving in OB leadership while her male counterpart, at best, is ambivalent about how Scripture portrays women in relation to the OB role. The need for conversation is also suggested by the difference in how a significant number of male minister respondents view the relationship between family and questions about the church leadership of women. Of the nearly 40 percent of those OB respondents who saw a reason other than scriptural teaching as prohibiting women serving with them, most cited negative consequences for the "God-ordained order of the home . . . and society." At work in this rationale may be found the earlier mentioned "family values" agenda and a belief that fuller empowerment of women in the church violates tradition— an ironic but not frequent argument in some Pentecostal debates.[5] This convoluted reading of Scripture, where the arenas of church and home are merged and tradition cited is not upheld by New Testament scholars within Pentecostalism or the COG, and is not congruent with how women read the same texts.

Fifth, the Pentecostal female minister needs a support system where she may flourish instead of languishing in isolation. She needs more visible positive ministry role models and intentional provision for meaningful participation in state and denominational ministerial functions. She and her sisters need to feel respected and welcomed as a result of the use of gender

---

4. See Sandberg, *Lean In*, and Zenger and Folkman, "Gender Shouldn't Matter."

5. COG General Council OB discussions have involved the invoking of earlier precedents to forestall fuller ministry authority for women. Male debaters have actually posed the question of the issue as "Were our forefathers wrong?" This is an ironic argument for Pentecostals who reacted against tradition in their earliest days.

inclusive language and depictions of women in leadership roles in denominational publications. Contributions of women writers in serious publications on ministry leadership, beyond articles on local church "women's ministry" or the role of the pastor's wife, should be prominent.

Sixth, she needs to experience the healing and renewal that would come with public repentance for male domination by the denomination's male ministers. Such a confession in a corporate solemn assembly should involve district, state, and denominational levels and should account for past and present injustices in compensation, placement, and advancement. In addition, an aggressive restitution program for redress of the lack of provision of sufficient remuneration, as well as the opportunity for meaningful ministry placement and for advancement as ministers, should be implemented. The economic and vocational oppression of women ministers in the COG is a serious blight on the claim of the denomination to be either a Holiness or a Pentecostal body, much less part of a Holiness Pentecostal Movement. Such a public confession was made by a sister denomination, the International Pentecostal Holiness Church, in 1996. A part of that extensive confession stated,

> We, the men of the Pentecostal Holiness Church, confess that we have not honored the precedent set forth in God's Word. Often, we have not treated our wives as equal partners in marriage and ministry. We have distorted the doctrine of holiness by focusing on the external appearance of women. We recognize the sin of male domination and acknowledge that we have withheld from women places of honor in the church. We have not affirmed the ministries of qualified women by releasing them to serve in places of leadership. We also have shown inequity regarding their wages.[6]

6. International Pentecostal Holiness Church, "Solemn Assembly," para. 61.

Seventh and finally, she should be recognized as a strategic missional partner for the challenges of twenty-first-century ministry. Given the high level of involvement of women in church planting, evangelistic ministry, and the growing population of younger women pursuing advanced theological education compared to men, the hope of effective future mission will likely be determined by the church's willingness and action to support, bless, and commission women for greater ministry leadership.[7] Despite women's confidence in their call, abilities, and experience, there is no doubt they have been negatively affected emotionally and economically by the limitations imposed on them by the attitudes of male ministers, the lack of denominational support, and the lack of receptivity to women as pastors in congregations. The alarming diminishing number of women under the age of thirty holding ministerial credentials calls for a concerted effort to recruit, support, and strategically place women in viable and prominent ministry positions in Pentecostal ministry in the COG.

7. Sadly, most denominational efforts at training and encouraging church planters do not appear to acknowledge women as experienced church planters. A recent conference sponsored by US/Canada Missions failed to feature any women speakers ("USA/Canada Missions," https://www.faithnews. cc/?p=24263).

Chapter 7

Looking In from the Outside

CYNTHIA WOOLEVER
Research Director of US Congregations Project,
Presbyterian Church (USA), Louisville, KY

INTRODUCTION

WOMEN IN PUBLIC MINISTRY face many of the same joys and challenges that men in that role do, but they also face unique hardships. Few national studies of how Pentecostal or conservative Protestant women experience ministry exist. The Church of God Women in Ministry Survey represents the first national profile of this large group of ministers and sheds much needed light on their experience serving the church.

Instead of beginning with a small sample, the researchers utilized the universe of all 3,088 licensed women COG ministers in the United States. After obtaining email contact information for almost 2,400 of these clergy, 726 women completed the survey. Thus, the following findings are based on almost one in four of the total population of COG women ministers. That is an extraordinarily large national sample. The breadth of women responding further supports the representativeness of this study. Women ministers comprised of all age groups and living in forty-five states completed the survey. Besides the age range, this broad geographic representation (given that COG congregations are concentrated in about a dozen southern states) gives even more validity to the study results than many surveys.

For example, the researchers also compared the experiences and views of male COG ministers with women in ministry. For this part of the study, a random sample of 1,000 male ministers was drawn. Out of this modest number, only 160 men in ministry returned a survey. That is less than one in five from the small sample. Compared to the robustness of the female sample, the small number of male respondents means that any interpretation of male views must be regarded with some caution.

WHAT FACTORS INFLUENCE CHURCH OF GOD POLICIES ON WOMEN IN MINISTRY?

Five factors seem to drive the Church of God practices and policies with regard to the role of women in ministry. The study digs into each of these dynamics and attempts to uncover the difficulty they present for moving toward greater support for COG women clergy.

Theology-driven understandings. In the study, both male and female ministers are asked to express their beliefs about the nature of God and his work in the world. Surprisingly, both groups hold similar views about the mission of the church and the role of clergy.

Bible-driven understandings. The reading of Scripture and its interpretation is central to both groups as they express their beliefs about the authority and power of the pastoral office.

Spirit-driven understandings. All participants make frequent reference to seeking and deriving direction from prayer or discernment that comes from a sense of being led by God's Spirit.

Tradition-driven understandings. The COG has a rich heritage related to women's participation in ministry. How women in public ministry have been involved in the past informs current conversations about the future of women in ministry.

Data-driven understandings. Another perspective about what motivates women to enter ministry, what they experience, and what they contribute is drawn from documenting their current reality. The survey data offers basic information about the who, what, and how regarding COG female clergy and provides another way to explore what it means for women to be in public ministry.

THEOLOGICAL PERSPECTIVES

Not surprising given that both groups are in the COG, the findings make clear that male and female ministers are conservative in their theological and political thinking. Three in four women support the priority of male spiritual and decision-making leadership in the home, the traditional view of domestic gender roles. However, a significant minority of women ministers (17 percent) feel women should have a voice with men in making final decisions in the home. But when the focus shifts to spiritual matters, more female than male clergy believe that men and women should share equal *spiritual* responsibility and leadership in the home.

The research indicates that women place more emphasis on the responsibility of all Christians—male and female—to be part of God's work in the world. Coming from a theological understanding, women are open to seeing this responsibility and accountability as extending to leadership roles in the church.

SCRIPTURAL AND SPIRIT-FILLED PERSPECTIVES

The majority of men and women appear to arrive at different understandings of ministry based on how they read and interpret Scripture. Sociologist Jackson Carroll describes three complementary models of ministry, all of which are theologically and biblically supported.[1] Women ministers tend to emphasize one of these models more than the other two. This may be because they have been denied access to some aspects of ministry.

Ministry as Office

One of Carroll's ministry models posits pastoral leadership as an office or formal position in the church. The office has "official" duties, is recognized by ordination, and gives the office holder authority and power granted by the institution (in this case, the church). Women in COG ministry have been granted ordination and the right to serve as leaders in the local church. The denomination's understanding of women's leadership, however, limits their claim to ministry as an office exclusively to the local level. The current understanding excludes them from authority and leadership at the state, regional, or denominational level. The majority of women ministers participating in the survey felt that, in contrast to the denomination's view, Scripture was consistent with women assuming ministry and leadership at all levels. Male clergy respondents, however, tended to see that women serving at the state or national level was inconsistent with the COG tradition.

Ministry as Profession

Carroll's second ministry model places emphasis on the minister as an educated and competent professional. In this model, clergy are seen as responsible for acquiring the skills and background to competently carry out the core tasks of the pastoral office. The idea of ministry as a profession arose in the nineteenth century alongside other fields that developed special areas of expertise, such as lawyers and teachers.

The research shows that women are not supported in most of the steps required to become a minister with professional skills. In

1. Carroll, *God's Potters*, 16–25.

general, women are not sponsored or encouraged to enter ministry once they begin the process for training and ordination. Even after clearing those hurdles to ministry, women are often not allowed access to educational events that would further their acquisition of ministry competencies, as these opportunities are only offered to male clergy.

Ministry as Calling

The research found that COG women in ministry emphasize their sense of call to be a minister. First, many women believe that God has summoned or invited them to take up the work of ministry. Second, women believe that others recognize in them the gifts and talents that make them effective in ministry. In this model of Carroll's, others recognize an individual as having a call if she or he manifests a Spirit-filled life, exhibits spiritual depth, possesses high character, has a passionate commitment to God, and holds a strong vision for transforming people and the world with the Gospel message. COG women and men that see their ministry as a calling are not easily deterred by obstacles or lack of opportunity. Rather, those who are called believe God will provide the means for equipping them to do the ministry he has called them to do.

The study yields no evidence that casts doubt on the sincerity of women's call to ministry or on their capabilities to serve the church as leaders.

Each of these models of ministry highlights some aspect that various groups see as essential to effective ministry. For women in COG ministry, their sense of ministry as calling—the one aspect of ministry that is most personal and spiritual—grounds their work in ministry. Unfortunately, their lack of access to the office and professionalism of ministry inhibits their ministry from being all that it could contribute to the church.

TRADITIONAL PERSPECTIVES

The earliest beginnings of the Pentecostal movement, prior to 1912, included women as full partners in the effort to ignite a renewed gospel message. However, as time went by, some leaders were influenced by Evangelical and Fundamentalist groups' interpretations about the role of women at home and in the church. By 1931, women and men were fully segregated in COG church ministry, as only men could conduct church business and administration. In 1948, women officially retained their COG ministry role of "Evangelist," but were cut off from recognition as professional clergy. It was not until 2000 that COG women were effectively granted ordination. Even then, they were still excluded from the highest ministry rank of OB.

Despite the fluid boundaries between women's full participation in ministry over the past one hundred years, women's gifts for proclaiming the gospel were never denied or officially negated. This alone suggests that cultural understandings about women as ministry leaders more dramatically blocked their access to full equality in ministry than any consistent application of a biblical interpretation.

DATA-DRIVEN PERSPECTIVES

The Women in Ministry survey makes its strongest contribution in describing the current reality of women's experience in ministry. Indeed, any recommendations about the future of COG ministry must take into account the present context.

What motivates women to seek full equality in ministry? The research fails to find evidence for any of the three possible motivations proffered by opponents as to why women in public ministry desire greater recognition and support.

- *A liberal, secular, or feminist agenda.* Three out of four women ministers self-describe as "conservative" in their political orientation. White women are the most likely to say they are conservative, followed by only slightly smaller percentages of Hispanic, African-American, or Caribbean women. The majority of women across all ethnic groups are conservative in their thinking. The research shows that their political orientation is identical to the COG men in ministry.

- *A rejection of a traditional view of family.* About three out of four women ministers support the priority of male spiritual and decision-making leadership. There is no evidence from their responses that their call to ministry stems from a desire to change family dynamics.

- *Advocacy for a greater role for women in society.* More than 90 percent of both the women and men surveyed believe women should serve in civic or governmental leadership. Since both men and women agree that women can contribute to public service, the research shows that this cannot be the exclusive reason for women's hopes for greater support in ministry.

What views do women ministers hold about their role in the COG? The survey findings show that three out of four women believe that they should be recognized as OBs. The percentage of women holding this view is highest among Hispanic respondents (96 percent). In general, the more education obtained by the respondent, the more likely she is to believe women should be OBs. A slim majority of men (54 percent) agree that women should be recognized as OBs. As with their female counterparts in ministry, the more educated men support women's recognition as OBs by larger margins.

How do women ministers interpret biblical teachings about female church leadership? Women ministers do not believe that Scripture teaches against women serving as OBs (80 percent hold this view). A slim majority of male ministers (56 percent) agree that women are not prohibited by Scripture from serving as OBs. An even higher percentage of women (90 percent) believe they should be able to vote in the GC (compared to 54 percent of men). Most women (87 percent) also feel they should be able to lead at the state or local level. However, only half of the male respondents supported women serving as leaders at the state or local level.

What are the reasons behind restricted access for women to some leadership roles? Men and women agree that women are capable of taking on administrative roles. Women express that there are "other reasons" behind the restrictions. The "other reason" women cite most often is "the difficulty that some men have with women in leadership." In contrast, male ministers (70 percent) say their objections stem from their understanding of biblical teachings.

Do women receive recognition and support for their ministry? The research frames this question in terms of what it means to flourish as a person in ministry. The respondents report that they receive more informal affirmation than formal or systemic support.

- *Informal support for women's ministry.* Almost all of the married women (94 percent) say their families support their work in ministry. The same is true of unmarried women, who make up about 25 percent of female clergy. Local congregations also give support by recognizing them as a minister (three out of four say this has happened) or giving them the opportunity to preach at their church (three out of four say this has happened). Most women (94 percent) said they have close friendships with other ministers. Often these were other women ministers. The study participants also named female role models that inspire them. The majority of named role models, however, were not actually women currently in ministry.

- *Formal support for women's ministry.* A second type of recognition comes from what the church as a system or institution does to legitimize women's call to ministry. The first step in the credentialing and ordination process involves the help of the woman's own pastor. Less than half (44 percent) of the women said they were sponsored by their pastor. In half of the cases, no explanation was given to the woman concerning why the pastor would not assist her in seeking credentialing or ordination. Only one in three received information from their local pastor about educational opportunities. Slightly less than half (49 percent) reported that their pastor prayed with them for discernment about their ministerial call.

At the district or state level, formal recognition of women's role in ministry is even less evident than on the local level. Women are rarely asked to keynote at conferences or to serve as workshop leaders. A minority (40 percent) have been asked to preach at state or denominational meetings. Because the majority of women ministers are, because of economic reasons, bi-vocational, they are able to participate less often in the State Ministers' Meetings (56 percent of women say they have attended compared to 83 percent of men). Only one in three have had the opportunity to attend a ministers' retreat (compared to 57 percent of men). Only at the denominational level do female and male ministers participate at roughly the same rates (about 34 percent in both groups).

HOW DO WOMEN MINISTERS COMPARE TO MEN IN COMPENSATION AND BENEFITS FOR THEIR MINISTRY SERVICE?

Receiving adequate salaries and benefits is another type of formal recognition indicating the value of women's ministry.

No compensation. More than 62 percent of women COG ministers serve without compensation. Another 3 percent make less than $5,000 annually. Even those women who receive compensation earn much less than what men earn. As the report indicates, 80 percent of women ministers earn less than $20,000 annually, while 80 percent of men GOC clergy earn more than $20,000 annually. Of the women who are compensated from other employment, a higher percentage (72 percent) receives no salary or wages from their ministry work. Of the men who receive compensation from other employment, only 15 percent receive no salary or wages from their work in ministry.

No housing allowance. Most women ministers (84 percent) do not receive a housing allowance. Only 40 percent of men do not receive this benefit. This is a benefit that has substantial income tax advantages.

No pension plan. Compared to receiving a housing allowance, even fewer women ministers can rely on retirement funds from their time in ministry (88 percent do not participate in a church or denominational pension plan). Slightly less than half (47 percent) of men do not participate in the denominational pension plan.

No full-time work in ministry. Whereas three out of four women serve part-time in ministry, only about 40 percent of men serve part-time. Also, the research found that women rarely serve as lead pastors. The most common positions held by women are evangelist (17 percent), teacher (12 percent), or associate pastor (11 percent). Almost all men (82 percent) are appointed to their church, but the majority of women (58 percent) must find their own place in ministry. The one open avenue to becoming a pastor is to plant a church—women are three times more likely to plant a church than men (48 percent compared to 16 percent).

Short ladders. There is little record of advancement for women. Those most able to gain full-time employment or a lead pastor position have more education (such as a college or more advanced degree). These women are also most likely to find placement and opportunities for ministry outside the local church setting.

CONCLUSION

This large representative portrait of women in COG ministry clarifies the different perspectives contributing to understanding the current status of women. From a theological standpoint, men and women are on the same page. Women strongly identify as

Pentecostal and embrace the conservative teachings of the church. Using Scripture as a lens to view women's role in ministry highlights the area where men and women are most likely to hold different views. Despite the diversity of interpretations, most women and the majority of men do not believe that Scripture prohibits women from any ministry role. Women are especially animated by their sense of calling and the discernment of the Spirit. Even men who do not fully support a greater role for women in church leadership do not question their passion and commitment to or their capabilities and gifts for their ministry. A traditionalist perspective offers a more contested landscape with regard to women in ministry. Early historical examples of female leadership contrast with the closing window of opportunities women have experienced in the past seventy years.

The data generated from women's responses call for action from church leaders. Without more formal recognition and involvement in church leadership, the most gifted women will seek ministry opportunities outside the church. Gifted ministers—male and female—determine the future growth of the denomination by planting new churches and nurturing the growth of small churches. Bi-vocational pastors can be seen as a denominational strength, providing able leadership to small churches that cannot financially support a full-time pastor. But these ministers—female and male—need access to training to effectively carry out core ministry tasks. Given the scale of the church's challenges, no denomination can dismiss without peril the contributions of thousands of women with a deep faith and willingness to serve their church.

Epilogue

THE JOURNEY OF THIS book began with the dual purposes of learning more about what is at stake in the limitations placed on Pentecostal women ministers in the COG and of giving voice to those women who are not allowed to speak in decision-making processes that shape their lives and ministries. The hope with the first publication of this volume was that its findings and stories would provoke a larger conversation about gender, patriarchy, and ministry. Presentations of the data in conferences and academic settings have resulted in many "me too" responses from women in other denominations. Reviews and citations of the research have noted its significance for understanding and addressing the disadvantaged status of all women in ministry.[1] These reviews also note the shared experience of these COG women with women ministers in other denominations, Pentecostal and beyond.[2] Yet, no meaningful conversation or serious dialogue has been initiated.

Any actions taken have been more of the garden variety "women's conference" response (or token appearances by prominent pastors' wives or a few high-profile women ministers in other

---

1. For instance, Mireya Alvarez utilizes the research in an analysis of Pentecostal women ministers in Latin America and concludes, "the cultural patterns of American evangelicalism and fundamentalism were imposed on Pentecostal churches to exclude women from public office" (Alvarez, "Attitude is Everything," 97).

2. See "James Bowers and Kimberly Alexander"; Lathrop, Review of *What Women Want*; Rios, "Do You Hear"; and Qualls, "What Pentecostal Women Want."

venues). No effort has begun in the COG to change the systemic problems suppressing women ministers at the grassroots. No effort to actually listen to women or involve them in the discussions has been undertaken. In fact, a case could be made that matters are now worse, not better. A commissioned "study" on titles, ranks, and women in ministry scheduled as a "report" in the 2018 COG General Council—where only male voices will be heard—illustrates the unlikelihood of any real action being taken to address the concerns raised in our research.

While questions still remain after our study, answers have emerged about what influences are and are not at work in the debate over the full empowerment of women ministers. Notably, we've learned that Pentecostal women ministers are not motivated by a secular feminist agenda, nor do they harbor a latent or overt intent to destroy traditional marriage or families. In fact, they overwhelmingly enjoy the support of spouses and other family as they pursue God's call to ministry. Our data and stories show that women ministers in no way undermine strong family life.

These women take seriously the authority of Scripture, but read it differently from many men ministers. The differences in how women read Scripture and articulate theology compared to men is an important spiritual, doctrinal, and missional issue that begs further study and conversation. Women ministers have been shown to support denominational leadership and congregational pastoral leadership preferences. Yet, they are simultaneously being negatively impacted by lack of sufficient advocacy and support on both these fronts. It is apparent that women ministers experience much pain and grief about such lack of affirmation.

They also distinguish in a spiritually, Pentecostal, and distinctively scriptural way family and church leadership roles, while most male ministers—seemingly influenced by a less Pentecostal and more fundamentalist and patriarchal culture wars vision of family—have not been able to do the same. Largely without protest of the decidedly privileged economic and political status of their male counterparts, these same women serve faithfully and at great personal sacrifice in many ministry contexts, but especially as evangelists, church planters and associate pastors. Which means, of course, they often help make possible the ministry achievements and economic rise of their male senior pastor peers without sharing equally in the benefits of such success.

In the face of such ministerial subordination and suppression, what explains such enduringly selfless and effective service to God and the kingdom as these women demonstrate? Time and again, the answer was clear in their stories: these Pentecostal women ministers have a sure call from God and will not be stopped! Of the exemplars of faith, the writer of Hebrews said, "the world did not deserve them." That's the feeling we have about these Pentecostal women ministers: "We don't deserve them." Surely, they deserve better—better recognition, better economic affirmation, better opportunities to fulfill the Spirit's call to her daughters. May we listen to them; learn from their pain, wisdom, and perseverance; and lean into a better future for God's mission together as equal partners.

Appendix 1

Limiting Liberty[1]

David G. Roebuck, PhD
Director, Hal Bernard Dixon, Jr. Pentecostal Research Center, Cleveland, TN

ESTABLISHING THE LIMITATIONS OF WOMEN MINISTERS

Eliminating the Office of Deaconess

THE FIRST RECORDED RESTRICTING of women in any aspect of ministry eliminated the office of deaconess and effectively concluded the issue of ordination for the Church of God. The third Assembly in 1908 had recognized the office of deaconess and outlined duties for those women called and qualified. The denomination reversed this position at the very next Assembly, however. Under the subject "Female ministers—Deaconesses and Evangelists," the 1909

---

1. The following material is taken with only slight modification from the work of David G. Roebuck, "Limiting Liberty." Here Roebuck establishes the historical process by which the Church of God limited women to the office of Lady Evangelist. This limitation remained in effect until 1990.

Please note that the sources cited in this essay do not have full citations in the bibliography of this book.

Assembly acknowledged that female ministers existed in the time of the apostles, and that the church must continue to recognize them. This Assembly also established a single license for women "who engage in the ministry of the word" and for "unordained male ministers,"[2] thereby creating the office of evangelist.

At the same time, however, the third Assembly eliminated the office of deaconess. The diaconate was an ordained order of ministry, and apparently women serving in this office were a problem for some in the Church of God. As was its practice, the Assembly referred to the Bible for answers. According to the Assembly, there was no example of the ordination of female ministers in the New Testament. Therefore, "for the present . . . the wives of the deacons [shall] be considered and appointed deaconesses by virtue of the position and ordination of their husbands."[3] The Assembly was unwilling to suggest that there should not be deaconesses. Yet the office of deacon was an ordained position, and they could find no New Testament example of the ordination of a woman. This solution allowed them to continue the office while holding to their understanding of ordination.

Although the decision seemingly allowed for the office of deaconess to continue, the effect was the elimination of the office from actual practice. There is no evidence that women were officially recognized as deaconesses from that time forward. An examination of the minutes of the North Cleveland (Tennessee) church revealed the practice of one local congregation. These minutes, which exist from 1910 and are the oldest local Church of God minutes available, denoted in the membership record the ministerial status, if any, of each member. Several bishops, deacons and evangelists were members of this leading congregation in the denomination. Although the minutes indicated which women were evangelists, there was no notation of any deaconess. Wives of deacons followed the names of their husbands without any acknowledgment of ministerial office for the women. Thus, within

2. *General Assembly Minutes 1906–1914*, 63.
3. *General Assembly Minutes 1906–1914*, 63.

one year of the shift to marriage as the primary qualification, no women were being identified as deaconesses.[4]

The Examination Certificate that ministerial candidates completed provides additional evidence that the office of deaconess ceased to exist. The form itself was inconsistent in its recognition that women might be applicants. Some of the questions referred to the candidate's spouse as "wife" but added "husband" in parentheses, while other questions did not add "husband." The instructions for completing this form emphasized the importance of the office of bishop and the office of deacon. In both cases, the wife of the minister was required to measure up to a particular standard. Although the office of deacon "is much more exalted than has been recognized by many of the modern churches," there was no mention of the wife holding the office of deaconess.[5]

Finally, when the denomination codified the rulings of the Assemblies into a Supplement to the minutes in 1931, there was no indication of the existence of deaconesses. All previous discussions regarding deaconesses were omitted at that time from the sections related to deacons and female ministers.[6]

Excluding Women from Ordination

The 1908 decision to exclude women from being ordained as deaconesses also set the continuing precedent for excluding women from ordination. The Assembly concluded that there was no New Testament example of the ordination of a woman. Consequently, "for the present," they were unwilling to ordain women. The minutes did not record whether the denomination had ordained any women, or whether and how any ordained deaconesses would have their ordination revoked. The fact that the minutes were silent

4. *Minutes of the North Cleveland Church of God 1910-1942*, Hal Bernard Dixon Jr. Pentecostal Research Center, Cleveland, Tennessee.

5. Examination Certificate of Lulu Jones, dated March 18, 1916. The staff of the Office of Central Files at the Church of God International Offices indicated that this application form was the earliest form of which they were aware.

6. *Minutes of the 26th Annual Assembly*, 108-9.

on these issues, as well as any rationale used during the previous year to ordain women, may suggest that no women were actually ordained.

This ruling clearly did allow for women to be licensed "to engage in the ministry of the Word."[7] However, it placed them in the same category as unordained licensed men—a category in which they remained. During the succeeding years, the authority of licensed female evangelists was variable for a time, then was increasingly limited, and finally was equated with that of licensed men.

Limiting the Rights and Authorities of Evangelists

Recent acquisition of copies of many ministerial certificates has allowed for a clearer understanding of the process that excluded women from ministerial rights and authorities, such as baptism, administering the Lord's Supper, and the washing of the saints' feet. Previous interpreters relied on the minutes of the annual Assemblies, especially the Twentieth Assembly in 1925, which specifically discussed the limits of female evangelists. When the Committee on Questions was asked if they were "going to allow a woman Evangelist to administer the Lord's Supper, feet washing, baptism, etc.," their succinct answer was "No."[8] Noting that

7. *General Assembly Minutes 1906-1914*, 63. At this time, most recognition of ministers was still taking place in the local church. These female ministers, as well as unordained male ministers, were to be "acknowledged by the church and supplied with a certificate or license showing the date of appointment and by what church." At least the second reference to "church" was to a local church.

8. *Minutes of the Twentieth Annual Assembly 1925*, 40. The word "etc." was not explained, but at a later time men were given the right to solemnize marriages and establish churches, while women were not given these rights and authorities. J. H. Ingram was called to organize the first Church of God in Mexico and to baptize the first members there. It was one of the congregations already established by Maria Atkinson. When Margaret Gaines was ready to organize a Church of God in Tunisia, she traveled to Germany by ship and train to find the closest male missionary, Lambert DeLong. She convinced him to come to Megrine, where he organized the first Church of God congregation in Tunisia on August 25, 1957. See Ingram, "Pioneering in Mexico," 9; and

the Assembly minutes had not recorded separate licenses until the introduction of a Supplement in 1931, previous interpreters suggested that this 1925 question and answer led to the printing of a separate license for women.[9] The licenses cited in 1931 did not arise out of the 1925 question-and-answer session, however. Recent acquisition by the Hal Bernard Dixon, Jr. Pentecostal Research Center of a large number of ministerial credentials gave the opportunity for a fresh

---

Conn, *Where the Saints,* 277.

9. See Dirksen, "Let Your Women"; Webb, "Limitations," 24; and Stone, "Ministerial Development," 95–96. In his recounting of these events, Stone concluded that, because there was no official Assembly business item forbidding women from sacerdotal functions, this question and answer had the import of setting the tradition that would prevail in the Church of God. According to Stone, this influenced the printing of separate licenses for women evangelists—licenses that did not forbid, but did not include the authority to baptize, marry, and officiate in the Lord's Supper and feet washing. Stone cited the licenses that were quoted in the Supplement to the minutes in 1931.

Further, Stone suggested that, although this limitation of women's roles became the accepted practice of the Church of God, it should not have become such. He noted that at the same Assembly the question was raised concerning vaccinations and the answer was that vaccinations should be avoided. According to Stone, "There is no more justification for accepting one of these statements as the official policy of the General Assembly of the Church of God than for accepting the other" (132n54). He went on to cite the twenty-fourth Assembly that stated, probably in reaction against Tomlinson who had been impeached, "Resolved, that we, the Church of God, do not consider the questions and answers, which answers were given by an individual and not approved by the General Assembly in session, as any part of the teachings or government of the Church of God." (*Minutes of the Twenty-Fourth Annual Assembly 1929,* 35).

Actually, the answer given in 1925 was given by a committee appointed by the Assembly rather than by a single individual, so it was not excluded by the motion of the Twenty-Fourth Assembly. Additionally, such questions and answers tended to reflect the attitudes of the Assembly at that time. Although later interpreters may question the lack of parliamentary procedure, it appears that the Assembly in 1925 agreed with the outcome. Regarding health concerns, most of the denomination rejected the use of medical attention by a physician. In 1929, General Overseer F. J. Lee died of cancer without medical attention (see Conn, *Like a Mighty Army,* 202). Although Stone may regret the fact that women were excluded from these sacerdotal rites, this dissertation demonstrates that limiting the authorities of women reflected the attitude of the Assembly at that time.

examination of the question of rights and authorities of women ministers. With these additional documents, it is evident that limitations of women's ministerial authorities occurred earlier than previously thought. Indeed, the restrictions noted in 1925 and the authorities recorded in the 1931 Supplement had actually been in vogue since 1914. The practice that the Church of God had followed since 1914 of distinguishing between the authorities of male and female evangelists was affirmed in the 1925 question-and-answer meeting and then specifically listed in the 1931 Supplement to the minutes.[10] This was evidence of what happens so often in the formation of denominational polity—official polity tends to follow rather than precede practice.[11]

Early evangelist licenses varied in their authorization. The second Assembly granted an evangelist license to H. L. Trim in 1907 and agreed "to use the printed form all ready [sic] in use by some."[12] This version of the evangelist license gave the evangelist the authority to "publish, preach and defend the Gospel of Jesus Christ as taught by the Holy Apostles." It then included a blank line on which additional responsibilities were sometimes written. Although this form of the license did not identify the gender of an evangelist, overseers sometimes added sacerdotal responsibilities

10. The Supplement was a collection of excerpts from previous minutes which give "all acts and teachings now in vogue" (*Minutes of the Twenty-Sixth Annual Assembly 1931*, 90).

The 1931 Supplement seems to have been based in part on a tradition of books intended to serve as guides to ministers and/or members. These included Church of God, *Book of Doctrines*; Church of God, *Book of General Instructions*; and Church of God, *Book of General Instructions . . . "Book Two."* The 1929 *Book of General Instructions* stated that the women evangelists had a "special license adopted to their work" (*"Book Two,"* 26).

Dirksen suggested that the changes in licenses were made at the Twenty-First Assembly in 1926. She cited page 109; but this page number matched the 1931 Supplement rather than the 1926 minutes ("Let Your Women," 174)

11. R. Hollis Gause, author of *Church of God Polity* and long-time parliamentarian of the General Council and General Assembly suggested that policy follows rather than precedes practice in many aspects of Church of God polity. See Gause, "Development of General Polity."

12. *General Assembly Minutes 1906–1914*, 65.

to men's licenses, while there is no evidence that they ever added them to women's licenses.[13]

Another form of the evangelist license that the denomination issued between 1909 and 1914 gave the evangelist authorization to "publish, preach and defend the Gospel of Jesus Christ, to baptize, to administer the Lord's Supper and the washing of the Saints feet."[14] Although both men and women received this license, there is no evidence that women actually officiated in a baptismal or communion service.[15]

The Church of God clearly delineated separate authorities for male and female evangelists in 1914, however. The earliest example of this that I have been able to find is the license of Pearlie J. Creel. Her license was the same as that mentioned above. The printed license authorized the evangelist to "publish, preach and defend

13. See evangelist licenses issued to H. L. Trim (January 12, 1907), William R. Hadsock (October 24, 1909), W. M. Murphy (January 29, 1910), O. M. Moody (May 31, 1910), C. M. Ellard (January 29, 1911), Lorena Cotton (January 29, 1911), and Eva Padgett (1912). The comments on the licenses of Trim, Hadsock, and Murphy were "Also to Baptize, Administer the Lord's Supper and Washing the Saints [sic] feet." Moody's additional comments included "and also to baptise [sic]," but Ellard's and Cotton's added "and is recomended [sic] to the love and fellowship of the saints" without any mention of baptism, even though Ellard is male and Cotton is female. Padgett's license did not have any additional comments.

My initial observation is that the additional comments depended on the person who signed the license. Tomlinson signed the licenses of Trim, Hadsock, and Murphy, which included most authorities, but he did not grant sacerdotal authorities to the two women. These licenses are on file at the Hal Bernard Dixon, Jr. Pentecostal Research Center in Cleveland, Tennessee.

14. See the evangelist licenses of Rebecca Barr (May 31, 1910), Mrs. Nora Chambers (August 20, 1910), Esthill H. Cecil (July 1, 1911), Mrs. J. R. Elliott (June 1, 1912), W. A. Walker (July 4, 1912), Mrs. Emma Underwood (July 28, 1912), Mamie Inglett (September 15, 1912)and Sister Elizabeth Anderson (March 15, 1913).

15. This is not a claim that no Church of God woman had ever officiated in a baptismal or communion service, but certainly it would not have been expected, as it was not the norm. There is a recorded example of Rebecca Barr apparently leading a feet washing service. She was with her husband and may have led the service under his supervision. See Barr, "They 'Shall See Visions,'" 6–7.

the Gospel of Jesus Christ, to baptize, to administer the Lord's Supper and the washing of the Saints feet." On her particular copy, however, a line was drawn neatly through the words "to baptize."[16] Some time during 1914, denominational leadership issued new evangelist credentials: one form for men and one for women. These certificates were identical except for the ministerial authorities granted. The license for men included the same authorities the Church of God had previously granted to evangelists.[17] The license for women was further limited, however. The license for women granted the evangelist the authority to "publish, preach and defend the Gospel of Jesus Christ; and do all the work that may devolve on her as a prophetess or female minister of the Gospel."[18] Thus, the 1931 Supplement simply recorded into the minutes—and thereby placed them into the official record—the practices that had been in vogue since 1914. These continued to be the authorities granted to women evangelists until 1990.

What prompted the 1925 question and answer regarding women's rights and authorities? It is possible that the lack of specific distinctions in an "official" book on church belief and practice, such as the 1922 *The Book of Doctrines*, may have prompted the question and answer at the 1925 Assembly. Licenses included the authorities granted to the minister, but did not specify those that the denomination denied. Although it was clear to the leadership granting the licenses that there were specific differences in the rights and authorities of male and female evangelists, these differences may not have been obvious to the entire church. Since *The*

16. See the evangelist license of Pearlie J. Creel (April 19, 1914). One might interpret the fact that the overseer did not strike the words "to administer the Lord's Supper and the washing of the Saints feet," to imply that she had these authorities. Although there is no evidence that a woman administered the Lord's Supper, one cannot conclude with absolute certainty that no overseer ever allowed it. Certainly the denomination specifically prohibited these by the end of that same year.

17. See as an example the evangelist license of James O. Sauls (July 28, 1914).

18. See as an example the evangelist license of Rachel J. Brackett (December 25, 1914).

Book of Doctrines did not deal with the issue, questions may have been raised which needed clarity at the Assembly level. This is not to suggest that there was strong disagreement on the subject. After all, the answer presented by the committee was accepted without discussion. The Assemblies continually affirmed the distinction between male and female evangelists. Due to the lack of bishops, the Church of God appointed some evangelists as pastors. The Twentieth Assembly in 1925 decided to allow evangelists serving as pastors to have the authority to solemnize matrimony in those cases where the state allowed it. The Assembly agreed that an explanation of this fact should be attached to the evangelist license.[19] Certainly, in 1925 there was no suggestion that women be allowed to solemnize marriages.[20] Additionally, the denomination excluded women from a 1943 expansion of the responsibilities of male evangelists. At that time, "colored" bishops and male evangelists were given the opportunity to express their preference for their state overseer. Apparently, white male bishops already had this privilege. The fact that women evangelists were not given this privilege further

19. *Minutes of the Twentieth Annual Assembly 1925*, 38. For males, this was in part a reversal of a 1913 statement by the Eighth Assembly regarding evangelists. At the Eighth Assembly, one question asked why deacons and evangelists could not solemnize marriage. After lengthy discussion, the Assembly recalled that the licensing of deacons and evangelists had been instituted because there were some who did not have the ability to solemnize marriages. According to the Eighth Assembly, only bishops should be granted the right to solemnize marriages. Indeed, those who advanced in the ministry to the point of being able to solemnize marriages "would usually be able to be ordained a Bishop." H. Lynn Stone noted that this statement implied that only males would progress to the point of being able to solemnize marriages since only males could be ordained bishops. See *General Assembly Minutes 1906–1914*, 228; and Stone, "Ministerial Development," 94.

In 1972, exhorters who served as pastors of churches were given the right to solemnize marriages. Thus, males who were part of a office lower than that of evangelist could do something that a woman could not do. *Minutes of the 54th General Assembly 1972*, 46.

20. The "etc." of the 1925 Assembly may have been referring to solemnizing marriages when it negatively answered the question, "Are we going to allow a woman Evangelist to administer the Lord's Supper, feet washing, baptism, etc.?"

distinguished them from their male counterparts.[21] Then in 1944 the Assembly affirmed that only men could administer the rite of baptism. In a paragraph in the Supplement to the minutes referring to water baptism, the Assembly deleted the words "Women evangelists are not allowed to administer water baptism" and replaced them with "That water baptism be administered by ordained or licensed male ministers."[22] In 1946, the Assembly further enhanced the position of male evangelists by encouraging their ordination if they had been involved in ministry for four years. This 1946 ruling hinted at the changes in ministerial offices that would occur at the next GA in 1948.[23]

The Church of God also placed financial limitations on women ministers that it did not place on their male colleagues. In 1950 the Assembly limited the pension of a female minister, if her family had not depended on her as their principal means of support, to only one-half of that of a male minister whose family had depended on his ministerial income as their primary means of support. Additionally, the Assembly said that it had always been the custom to grant only one pension when both husband and wife were ministers.[24]

21. *Minutes of the 38th Annual Assembly 1943*, 31.

22. *Minutes of the 39th General Assembly 1944*, 30. This appears to be part of an effort to clean up the section on baptism rather than a specific focus of attention on women. The wording under the section on female ministers went unchanged.

23. "That licensed male evangelists, who have had four years of service and are at present actively engaged in either pastoral or evangelistic work be ordained, if found eligible and that future applicants for the ministry be required to serve as exhorters for a period of one year of active service in the ministry before they will become eligible to be licensed or ordained evangelists." The phrase "ordained evangelists" was not explained. It may have referred to ordained bishops who were not pastors. The 1948 and 1950 minutes listed the numbers of ministers by office, with 242 and 221 ordained evangelists respectively. In 1950, the Assembly ruled: "That ordained evangelists who are eligible for ordained ministers' license be promoted and those who are not eligible be given licensed ministers' certificates" (*Minutes of the 41st Assembly 1946*, 27; *Minutes of the 42nd Assembly 1948*, 34; and *Minutes of the 43rd General Assembly 1950*, 14, 26).

24. *Minutes of the 43rd General Assembly 1950*, 16–17. The idea that a wife

Although the license for female ministers had not included the right to solemnize marriages, the Assembly codified that exclusion in 1952 by adding it to the existing statement of exclusions. According to the amended statement, "The female ministers are not allowed to administer baptism, Lord's Supper, feet washing, solemnize the rights of matrimony, etc."[25] This exclusion was not new. Certificates for male evangelists and later licensed ministers clearly gave them the right to solemnize marriages,[26] although the certificates for female ministers had omitted this authority. This represented an increasing codification of the limitations of women ministers.[27]

At the next Assembly in 1954, the paragraph granting women the right to serve as "helpers or assistant pastors" of district overseers was deleted from the section of minutes referring to female ministers. The Assembly did not explain why the deletion was made, however.[28] This item was originally adopted in 1913 as part of the organization of the church into districts, which were admin-

---

did not need financial support continued to pervade the Church of God. One woman reported to me that she had never received an offering for preaching in her local church, although men who preached always received an offering. Personal files of the author, Cleveland, TN.

25. *Minutes of the 44th General Assembly 1952*, 32. Note that in the Supplement, the word "etc." was not included and the citation remained the Twentieth Assembly rather than the Forty-Fourth Assembly (*Minutes of the 44th General Assembly 1952*, 216).

26. Male evangelists and licensed ministers had been able to solemnize marriages if they were pastors. In 1956, the Forty-Sixth Assembly gave all licensed ministers the right to solemnize marriages (*Minutes of the 46th General Assembly 1956*, 26).

27. Male evangelists who were serving as pastors had been given the right to solemnize marriages by the Twentieth Assembly (*Minutes of the 20th Assembly 1925*, 38).

28. *Minutes of the 45th General Assembly 1954*, 26. The paragraph that was deleted read: "The pastor or overseer of each district shall have helpers or assistant pastors, who shall be under his supervision, for the care of the care of the churches of the district. These helpers may include WOMEN PREACHERS and evangelists. Provisions for the support of these helpers may be determined by the overseer of the state and pastor of the district in joint conference" (*Minutes of the 44th Assembly 1952*, 216).

istered by district pastors or overseers. Yet this reference to helpers or assistant pastors was not included when the duties of the district overseer were first itemized in the 1944 Supplement. There probably had never been many assistant district overseers and this 1954 deletion may have been an attempt to delete from the minutes an item that was no longer in vogue rather than an attempt to limit the role of women ministers. Whatever the reason for the deletion, it resulted in one less specified role for women ministers.[29]

THE EVOLVING OFFICE OF "LADY EVANGELIST"

Significant in the process of limiting the roles of women in the Church of God was the gradual separation of women into a category of their own—that of "lady evangelist." Although the office itself was never officially discussed or created by the GA, the nomenclature became such a common part of the language of the denomination that it was eventually incorporated into the official documents of the denomination.

The gradual move toward identifying women as "lady evangelists" began with the 1931 Supplement which quoted the separate ministerial certificates of male and female evangelists that the denomination had used since 1914. Besides noting those distinct credentials, this Supplement actually placed women in a separate class of ministry with its listing of ministerial offices. When discussing these offices, the Supplement listed the heading of "MINISTERS" followed by the office that was being explained. Instead of listing and discussing four categories—Bishops, Deacons, Evangelists and Exhorters—the Supplement listed five groups: Bishops, Deacons, Evangelists, Female, and Exhorters.[30] Although the list of ministers included in the minutes still combined male and female

29. See *Minutes of the Thirteenth Annual Assembly 1917*, 35–36; and *Minutes of the 39th Annual Assembly 1944*, 162.

30. Furthermore, although the license quoted for the "Female" referred to the minister as an "Evangelist" and as a "prophetess," the Supplement used all capital letters to highlight the words "FEMALE MINISTER" (*Minutes of the 26th Annual Assembly 1931*, 93).

evangelists into one list, women clearly were a distinct category of ministers by 1931.[31]

The Assembly made broadly sweeping changes to the ministerial offices in 1948. It abolished the office of deacon and recalled all deacons' credentials.[32] It changed the title for the office of bishop to "ordained minister" and the title for the office of evangelist to "licensed minister." Additionally, it established age and years of service requirements for promotion from licensed minister to ordained minister. According to the Assembly, however, "It is understood that the ministerial status of lady evangelists remains unchanged."[33] What the Assembly meant by the reference to the status of "lady evangelists" is unclear. It was probably a reminder that they could not be ordained.

Although the minutes continued to list women among the licensed ministers, a shift occurred in the discussion of women in the Supplement. Previous Supplements had listed the discussion of female evangelist immediately following the discussion of evangelists in general, but the 1948 Supplement moved the discussion of women to the position following the discussion of exhorters. In this new arrangement, rulings listed under the heading "Licensed Ministers" apparently referred to men only. Thus, the reader had to move to the heading "Female" to learn anything about a woman minister. This clearly separated the discussion of women ministers from the discussion of male minister. Women in ministry were now outside the discussion of the three offices of male ministry, effectively relegating them to the roles of helper and evangelist.[34]

The fact that the Church of God viewed women ministers as a class separate from that of male licensed ministers was evident in the *Minutes of the 46th General Assembly*. Reporting on the

31. For the list of evangelists, see *Minutes of the 26th Annual Assembly 1931*, 57–63.

32. The Assembly ruled that the present order of deacons were unable to render proper service and allowed the pastor to annually select men who were qualified to counsel with the pastor and carry out the

33. *Minutes of the 42nd General Assembly 1948*, 27.

34. *Minutes of the 42nd General Assembly 1948*, 197.

memorial service at that Assembly in 1956, the minutes listed those ministers who had died during the preceding two years. Technically, only three offices existed at that time: ordained, licensed, and exhorters. Yet four categories of ministers were specified: ordained ministers, licensed ministers, evangelists, and exhorters. The list of licensed ministers included only male ministers and the list of evangelists included only female ministers.[35] This pattern of listing deceased men as licensed ministers and deceased women as evangelists continued until 1984. The separation between male ministers and female evangelists was clear.[36]

The Assembly officially codified the role of female minister as evangelist in 1958. The Forty-Seventh General Assembly organized and listed the qualifications, rights, and authorities of all offices of ministry for the first time. Four levels of ministry were listed: ordained minister, licensed minister, female minister, and exhorter. The qualifications, rights, and authorities for the female minister were:

Qualifications

1. Must have the baptism of the Holy Ghost.

2. The female candidate for the rank of evangelist shall be actively engaged in the ministry, either in evangelistic or pastoral work.

---

35. *Minutes of the 49th General Assembly 1956*, 5.

36. *Minutes of the 47th General Assembly 1958*, 13; *Minutes of the 48th General Assembly 1960*, 20; *Minutes of the 49th General Assembly 1962*, 15; *Minutes of the 50th General Assembly 1964*, 23; *Minutes of the 51st General Assembly 1966*, 27; *Minutes of the 52nd General Assembly 1968*, 32; *Minutes of the 53rd General Assembly 1970*, 30; *Minutes of the 54th General Assembly 1972*, 29; *Minutes of the 55th General Assembly 1974*, 24–25; *Minutes of the 56th General Assembly 1976*, 33; *Minutes of the 57th General Assembly 1978*, 33; *Minutes of the 58th General Assembly 1980*, 33–34; *Minutes of the 59th General Assembly 1982*, 39; and *Minutes of the 60th General Assembly 1984*, 34–35. There was no indication as to why women were included in the list of licensed ministers beginning in 1986. *Minutes of the 61st General Assembly 1986*, 33–34.

3. Must be thoroughly acquainted with the teachings and doctrines of the Church of God set forth by the General Assembly.

4. Must successfully pass the examination given by a duly constituted board of examiners.

Rights and Authorities

The female minister shall have full right and authority to:

1. Preach, publish, and defend the gospel of Jesus Christ.

2. Do the work of an evangelist.

3. Perform all the duties that may devolve on her as a prophetess[37] or female minister of the gospel.

4. Serve as pastor of a church under the supervision of the district pastor without authority to baptize converts, receive believers into fellowship of church membership, administer Holy Sacraments, or solemnize rites of matrimony.[38]

37. It is interested to note that the minutes did not refer to the male minister as a prophet.

38. *Minutes of the 47th General Assembly 1958*, 28–29. Compare these to those of the licensed minister:

Qualifications

1. Must have the baptism of the Holy Ghost.

2. The candidate for license minister shall be actively engaged in the ministry, either in pastoral or evangelistic work.

3. Must be thoroughly acquainted with the teachings and doctrines of the Church as set forth by the General Assembly.

4. Must successfully pass the examination given by a duly constituted board of examiners for ministerial candidates. It is understood that the examination will embrace areas of church government, doctrine, and general Biblical knowledge.

Rights and Authorities

The licensed minister shall have full right and authority to:

1. Preach, publish, teach, and defend the gospel of Jesus Christ.

2. Do the work of an evangelist.

The qualifications for licensed minister and female minister were very similar.[39] Yet, although candidates for both offices had to be involved in "either evangelistic or pastoral work," males were candidates for the office of licensed minister and females were candidates for the office of evangelist. Additionally, the rights and authorities of female ministers were specifically limited to proclamation activities. The female minister could not perform sacerdotal aspects of ministry and had to pastor under the supervision of a male district pastor. Also excluded without explanation from the rights and authorities of female ministers was the right to teach.[40]

In 1964, the minutes further extended the already existing practice of referring to women as evangelists. Until 1964, the minutes had continued to include women in the list of licensed ministers. At this time, the minutes changed the name of the former list entitled "Licensed Ministers" to "Licensed Ministers and Evangelists." Additionally, it included the notation "All ladies listed in this group are Evangelists" following this new heading.[41]

3. Serve as pastor of a church.

4. Baptize converts.

5. Receive believers into fellowship of church membership.

6. Administer Holy Sacraments.

7. Solemnize rites of matrimony.

8. Establish churches.

39. The main difference other than office was that, although both must pass an examination, the content of the examination for the licensed minister was specified: "It is understood that the examination must embrace areas of church government, doctrine and general Biblical knowledge" (*Minutes of the 47th General Assembly 1958*, 28–29).

40. The minutes did not make it clear what the right to teach meant. Nowhere did the Assembly actually prohibit women from teaching. Yet their certificates did not give them this right, whereas the certificates of male ministers did grant them the right to teach.

With this new codification of the offices of ministry, the order in which the Supplement listed the ministerial offices was harmonized with the new descriptions. For a short time, the description of the female followed that of the licensed minister and preceded the description of the exhorter (*Minutes of the 47th General Assembly 1958*, 30, 168–72).

41. *Minutes of the 50th General Assembly 1964*, 176. This practice ended in 1970 (*Minutes of the 53rd General Assembly 1970*, 210).

The 1964 Supplement made two additional changes regarding women ministers. It changed the heading of the section concerning women from "Female" to "Lady Minister." This probably represented a shift in what was considered the polite way to refer to women. This change in language seems to have been occurring for several years. The first use of the term "lady evangelist" had occurred in 1948 when the office of licensed minister was created.[42] The second change in the Supplement was a return to the earlier placement of the section referring to women. Once again, as it had before 1958, the section on women followed the discussion of the rank of exhorter, furthering the distinction between the licensed minister and the "lady minister."[43]

Finally, in 1972, the Church of God began to assign routinely the title "lady evangelist" to female evangelists on their credentials. This was done without action by the General Assembly, the Executive Council, or the Executive Committee. The certificates of "Lady Evangelists" read:

> This certifies that _____ is hereby appointed and commissioned as a Lady Evangelist in the Church of God with headquarters at Cleveland, Tennessee, U.S.A., to do the work of a Lady Evangelist and is hereby authorized to publish, preach and defend the gospel of Jesus Christ and do all the work that may devolve on her as a prophetess or female minister of the gospel.[44]

Although the remained the same, the Church of God now exclusively used the title "lady evangelist" to refer women ministers beyond the office of exhorter.[45]

42. *Minutes of the 42nd General Assembly 1948*, 27.

43. *Minutes of the 50th General Assembly 1964*, 3.

44. See the certificate of Dixie Chambers (documented at the Hal Bernard Dixon, Jr. Pentecostal Research Center). This certificate was dated February 21, 1932, but was a replacement certificate issued after 1972.

45. The Report of Ordination changed at this time as well. This card was sent from the state overseer to the General Offices in order to report the granting of credentials to any minister. During the early part of 1972, it listed three offices—ordained minster, licensed minister, and exhorter—along with a place

What had been a frequently used title to refer to women ministers was now firmly established as the official rank of the female minister beyond the apprentice stage of exhorter. The distinctions between the male and female minister were also determined. The male was a licensed minister and the female was a "lady evangelist."

---

for the overseer to check "his" or "her" depending on the gender of the minister. In late 1972, the denomination added the offices of licensed minister of music, licensed minister of C. E. and "lady evangelist" to the card. Then in 1972, the Church of God officially listed the office of "lady evangelist" for the first time on the forms used in the process of granting credentials. See cards issued for Juanita Joy Bradley (October 2, 1972) and Virginia Mae Montgomery (October 19, 1973) (documented at the Hal Bernard Dixon Jr. Pentecostal Research Center, Cleveland, Tennessee).

Appendix 2

Female Ministers in the United States

Demographic Profile

ETHNICITY

African-American	473	15%
Asian-American	13	0.004%
Hispanic	383	12.2%
Native American	28	0.009%
White (non-His)	1912	61%
Caribbean	329	10.4%
TOTAL	3138	

AGE

70+	509	15.3%	40-44	296	8.9%
65-69	332	9.9%	35-39	226	6.8%
60-64	414	12.4%	30-34	151	4.5%
55-59	459	13.8%	25-29	61	1.8%
50-54	504	15.1%	20-24	19	0.005%
45-49	354	10.6%	under 20	0	

Appendix 3

Pastor's Minimum Compensation Scale

(Effective September 1, 2012)

Please Note: These scales reflect the compensation and benefits from prior year (09/01/2011) due to no COL increase.

MEMBERS	WEEKLY COMPENSATION	MEMBERS	WEEKLY COMPENSATION
1–25	$781.00	326–350	$1,216.00
26–50	$830.00	351–375	$1,232.00
51–75	$875.00	376–400	$1,250.00
76–100	$919.00	401–425	$1,268.00
101–125	$964.00	426–450	$1,290.00
126–150	$1,011.00	451–475	$1,304.00
151–175	$1,056.00	476–500	$1,325.00
176–200	$1,105.00	501–525	$1,343.00
201–225	$1,118.00	526–550	$1,364.00
226–250	$1,141.00	551–575	$1,378.00
251–275	$1,158.00	576–600	$1,397.00
276–300	$1,177.00	601–625	$1,416.00
301–325	$1,194.00	626–650	$1,435.00

Pastor's Minimum Compensation Scale

MEMBERS	WEEKLY COMPENSATION	MEMBERS	WEEKLY COMPENSATION
651–675	$1,453.00	1151–1200	$1,842.00
676–700	$1,472.00	1201–1250	$1,875.00
701–725	$1,487.00	1251–1300	$1,912.00
726–750	$1,511.00	1301–1350	$1,951.00
751–775	$1,527.00	1351–1400	$1,984.00
776–800	$1,542.00	1401–1450	$2,021.00
801–825	$1,564.00	1451–1500	$2,061.00
826–850	$1,582.00	1501–1550	$2,094.00
851–875	$1,600.00	1551–1600	$2,134.00
876–900	$1,616.00	1601–1650	$2,168.00
901–925	$1,636.00	1651–1700	$2,025.00
926–950	$1,654.00	1701–1750	$2,243.00
951–975	$1,676.00	1751–1800	$2,280.00
976–1000	$1,689.00	1801–1850	$2,317.00
1001–1050	$1,728.00	1851–1900	$2,352.00
1051–1100	$1,763.00	1901–1950	$2,391.00
1101–1150	$1,800.00	1951–2000	$2,427.00

Churches with more than 2,000 members should follow the process of an increase of $20.00 per week in minimum salary for each increase of fifty members in continuing this scale.

Presently established churches whose pastor's salary structure is adversely affected by this scale should maintain their pastor's present compensation (observing annual adjustments) until membership has increased to a higher compensation bracket.

Bibliography

Alexander, Kimberly Ervin. "Pentecostal Women: Chosen for an Exalted Destiny." *Theology Today* 68.4 (2012) 404–412.

Alexander, Kimberly Ervin, and James P. Bowers. "Race and Gender Equality in a Classical Pentecostal Denomination: How Godly Love Flourished and Foundered." In *Godly Love: Impediments and Possibilities*, edited by Matthew T. Lee and Amos Yong, 131–51. Lanham, MD: Lexington, 2012.

Alexander, Kimberly Ervin, and R. Hollis Gause. *Women in Leadership: A Pentecostal Perspective*. Cleveland, TN: Center for Pentecostal Leadership and Care, 2006.

Alvarez, Mireya. "Attitude is Everything! Defending the Cause of Latin American Women in Ministry." In *The Reshaping of Mission in Latin America*, edited by Miguel Alvarez, 87–102. Vol. 30 of Regnum Edinburgh Centenary Series. Eugene, OR: Wipf and Stock, 2016.

Bessey, Sarah. "In Which I Am Done Fighting for a Seat at the Table." *Sarah Bessey* (blog), December 12, 2011. http://sarahbessey.com/in-which-i-am-done-fighting-for-seat-at/.

Bowers, James P., ed. *Portrait and Prospect: Church of God Pastors Face the Twenty-First Century*. Cleveland, TN: Center for Pentecostal Leadership and Care, 2004.

————. "Practices in the Spirit: A Pentecostal Model of Pastoral Formation." In *Passover, Pentecost & Parousia: Studies in Celebration of the Life and Ministry of R. Hollis Gause*, edited by Steven J. Land et al., 232–59. Vol. 36 of Journal of Pentecostal Theology Supplement. Dorset, UK: Deo, 2010.

Browning, Don S. "Toward a Fundamental and Strategic Practical Theology." In *Shifting Boundaries: Contextual Approaches to the Structure of Theological Education*, edited by Barbara G. Wheeler and Edward Farley, 295–328. Louisville: Westminster John Knox, 1991.

Bundy, David. Review of *Femmes et pentecôtismes: Enjeux d'autorité et rapports de genre*, by Gwendoline Malogne-Fer and Yannick Fer. *Pneuma* 38.1–2 (2015) 229.

"Bylaws of the Church of God." http://www.churchofgod.org/beliefs/bylaws.

Bibliography

Carroll, Jackson W. *God's Potters: Pastoral Leadership and the Shaping of Congregations*. Grand Rapids, MI: Eerdmans, 2006.

Carter, Nancy M. "Mentoring: Necessary but Insufficient for Advancement." http://www.catalyst.org/knowledge/mentoring-necessary-insufficient-advancement.

———. "Pipeline's Broken Promise." http://www.catalyst.org/knowledge/pipelines-broken-promise.

Chaves, Mark. *Ordaining Women: Culture and Conflict in Religious Organizations*. Cambridge: Harvard University Press, 1997.

Church of God. *Book of Doctrines*. Cleveland, TN: Church of God, 1922.

———. *Book of General Instructions for the Ministry and Membership*. Cleveland, TN: Church of God, 1927.

———. *Book of General Instructions for the Ministry and Membership, "Book Two."* Cleveland, TN: Church of God, 1929.

"Church of God Says Women Can't Be Bishops." *Christian Century*, August 27, 2010. http://https://www.christiancentury.org/article/2010-08/church-god-says-women-can-t-be-bishops.

English de Alminana, Margaret, and Lois E. Olena. *Women in Pentecostal and Charismatic Ministry: Informing a Dialogue on Gender, Church, and Ministry*. Global Pentecostal and Charismatic Studies 21. Leiden: Brill, 2016.

Fisher, Cameron. "Lee University Celebrates its Centennial in 2018." *Engage* (Winter 2018) 14–16. http://reader.mediawiremobile.com/PathwayPress/issues/202630/viewer.

Gause, R. Hollis. *Church of God Polity*. Cleveland, TN: Pathway, 1958.

———. "Development of General Polity." Lecture to the Church of God History and Polity class, Church of God School of Theology, Cleveland, TN, September 29, 1994.

Hilliard, Patricia. "Connecting Guests With the Church." *Engage* (Winter 2013) 14–15. http://reader.mediawiremobile.com/PathwayPress/issues/2979/viewer.

Ibarra, Herminia, et al. "Why Men Still Get More Promotions Than Women." *Harvard Business Review*, September 2010. https://hbr.org/2010/09/why-men-still-get-more-promotions-than-women.

International Pentecostal Holiness Church. "Solemn Assembly: Seizing the Future on our Knees." http://iphc.org/gso/archives/solemn-assembly/.

"James Bowers and Kimberly Alexander: Leadership and Women in Pentecostal Ministry." *Faith and Leadership*, January 27, 2014. https://www.faithandleadership.com/james-bowers-and-kimberly-alexander-leadership-and-women-pentecostal-ministry.

Knight, Michael. "Creating an Inviting Church Image." *Engage* (Winter 2013) 12. http://reader.mediawiremobile.com/PathwayPress/issues/2979/viewer.

Bibliography

Lathrop, John P. Review of *What Women Want: Pentecostal Women Ministers Speak for Themselves*, by James P. Bowers and Kimberly Ervin Alexander. *Priscilla Papers* 28.3 (2014) 30.

Malogne-Fer, Gwendoline, and Yannick Fer. *Femmes et pentecôtismes: Enjeux d'autorité et rapports de genre*. Geneva: Labor et Fides, 2015.

McDaniel, Anthony. "Family First, Church Second." *Engage* (Winter 2013) 28. http://reader.mediawiremobile.com/PathwayPress/issues/2979/viewer.

"Ministerial Licensure." http://www.cogdoe.org/ministries/ministerial-licensure-2/.

National Center for Education Statistics. "Median Annual Earnings of Year-Round, Full-Time Workers 25 Years Old and Over, by Highest Level of Educational Attainment and Sex: 1990 through 2010." http://nces.ed.gov/programs/digest/d11/tables/dt11_395.asp.

Qualls, Joy E. A. "What Pentecostal Women Want From Pentecostal Men." http://enrichmentjournal.ag.org/201403/201403_110_Pentecostal_Women.cfm.

Rios, Elizabeth D. "Do You Hear What I Hear?" http://www.evangelicalsforsocialaction.org/sexual-justice/do-you-hear-what-i-hear/.

Roebuck, David G. "'I Have Done the Best I Could': Opportunities and Limitations for Women Ministers in the Church of God—A Pentecostal Denomination." *Theology Today* 68:4 (January 1, 2012) 393–403.

———. "Limiting Liberty: The Church of God and Women Ministers, 1986–1996." PhD diss., Vanderbilt University, 1997.

Sandberg, Sheryl, and Nell Scovell. *Lean In: Women, Work and the Will to Lead*. New York: Knopf, 2013.

Shawyer, Tim W. "Engaging Senior Adults in Ministry." *Engage* (Winter 2013) 26. http://reader.mediawiremobile.com/PathwayPress/issues/2979/viewer.

Smidsrød, Ase-Miriam. "'For Such a Time as This': Gender Issues in Twenty-First Century Norwegian and Swedish Pentecostal Churches." *Pentecostudies* 15.2 (2016) 200–20.

Sollis, Hilda L., and Keith Hall. "Women in the Labor Force: A Databook." https://www.bls.gov/cps/wlf-databook-2011.pdf.

Spencer, Aída Besançon. "The View from the Pulpit: Honest Advice for Women in Ministry." https://www.cbeinternational.org/resources/article/mutuality/view-pulpit.

Stephenson, Lisa P. "Prophesying Women and Ruling Men: Women's Religious Authority in North American Pentecostalism." *Religions* 2 (2011) 410–26.

Swartz, Tony. "What Women Know about Leadership that Men Don't." *Harvard Business Review*, October 30, 2012. https://hbr.org/2012/10/what-women-know-that-men-dont.htm.

Thomas, John Christopher. "Biblical Reflections on Women in Ministry." In *Toward a Pentecostal Theology of Preaching*, edited by Lee Roy Martin, 135–40. Cleveland, TN: Centre for Pentecostal Theology, 2015.

Bibliography

———. "Women, Pentecostals and the Bible: An Experiment in Pentecostal Hermeneutics." *Journal of Pentecostal Theology* 5 (1994) 41–56.

Tomlinson, Ambrose J. *The Last Great Conflict*. Cleveland, TN: 1913.

———. "Paul's Statements Considered." *Church of God Evangel*, September 18, 1915.

"USA/Canada Missions Announces REWIRE Conference." *Faith News Network*, February 15, 2017. https://www.faithnews.cc/?p=24263.

Vrabel, Bjørg Marie Stubberud. "Kvinnelige eldste og forstandere? En undersøkelse av endringer I synet pa kvinnelige og forstandere I den norske pinsebevegelsen gjennom de siste hundre år" [Female Elders and Senior Pastors? An Examination of the Change of Views of Female Elders and Senior Pastors in the Norwegian Pentecostal Movement Over the Last Hundred Years]. Master's thesis, Det teologiske menighetsfakultet, Oslo, 2007.

Wagener, Linda M., and Richard Beaton. "Flourishing 101." *Theology, News and Notes* (Spring 2010). https://fullerstudio.fuller.edu/flourishing-101/.

Williams, Sandra Kay. "How a Pastor's Spouse Works with Staff." *Engage* (Fall 2017) 52–54. http://reader.mediawiremobile.com/PathwayPress/issues/201877/viewer.

Zenger, Jack, and Joseph Folkman. "Are Women Better Leaders than Men?" *Harvard Business Review*, March 15, 2012. https://hbr.org/2012/03/a-study-in-leadership-women-do.

———. "Gender Shouldn't Matter, But Apparently It Still Does." *Harvard Business Review*, April 4, 2012. https://hbr.org/2012/04/gender-shouldnt-matter-but-app?referral=00563&cm_mmc=email-_-newsletter-_-daily_alert.

Made in the USA
Coppell, TX
19 July 2021